55 OREGON BICYCLE TRIPS

BY NICK & ELSKE JANKOWSKI

map lettering:
BRIAN LIVINGSTON

THE TOUCHSTONE PRESS
P.O. BOX 81
BEAVERTON, OREGON 97005

Library of Congress
Catalog Card No. 73-80046
I.S.B.N. No. 0-911518-19-3

Introduction

Bicycling can be many things. It is the joy of feeling your legs pumping up and down as you speed forward. It is tears streaking across your face as you race down a steep hill. It is experiencing natural smells and sounds as you pedal through the countryside. It is achieving an inner solace, a restfulness — a kind of meditative sensation — while the wheels under you glide along the pavement. Bicycling is exercise — it gets the corpuscles circulating. Some people even see bicycling as a blow against pollution, a positive alternative to the automobile. But most of all, bicycling is fun. It is with these qualities in mind that we prepared this book of bicycle tours in Oregon.

There are 55 tours in this book. Many provide both short and long versions within the same area; therefore some 81 separate routes are charted on these pages. Most of the tours are loops of paved secondary roads, roads that automobile drivers have, for the most part, given up for the speedier concrete freeways.

These bike routes are concentrated in the Willamette Valley and along the Oregon Coast, from Lane County to the northern Oregon border. Two routes are in Clark County in Washington — routes Portlanders have easy access to. (A later volume will detail bicycle tours in southern and eastern Oregon.)

What are the ingredients of a good bicycle tour? An inexperienced rider might glance at the state highway map and conclude any road would be fine to bicycle. But there's much more to selecting a route than locating it on a map.

One of the primary considerations we made in selecting these tours was the traffic conditions along the routes. We avoided roads with heavy auto traffic. This was not always possible in the metropolitan areas, but once bicyclists are out of these central regions, traffic usually becomes negligible.

Road surface was another consideration in selecting bicycle routes. Only two routes have sections where the road is not paved with asphalt or other similar road covering. (These two routes have short sections of packed gravel.) The pavement on the tours in this book is of good to excellent quality.

The terrain of the bicycle routes is also important. We did not want to choose routes that were too hilly for the occasional bicyclist. This was not an easy task; much of this north-western corner of the state is more than hilly — it's downright mountainous! Consequently, there are a number of routes with climbs that the beginning rider may want to pass up. But we have also found a large number of easy-to-ride bicycle routes; these comprise the bulk of the tours in this book.

Whenever possible we tried to select routes that circled back to the starting point. A few of the routes, however, are single roads that must be bicycled both coming and going. But the majority of the tours are networks of roads forming loops.

Finally, the scenic value of a tour was considered. We tried to make a policy to have routes start either at parks or pass by a park along the way, to have a resting point. Again, this was not always possible, but most of the tours provide such facilities.

In addition, we looked for tours that had an attractive quality of another sort — a spectacular view, lush farmland, a landing along the river for wading or swimming, a meadow dotted with wildflowers. These qualities haven't been categorized and rated for each route; they are, by necessity, in the eyes of the beholder. They were in ours; we hope, when you bicycle the tours, they are in yours.

WILLAMETTE VALLEY

ontents

PORTLAND
METROPOLITAN AREA

THE OREGON COAST

How to Use the Book

Each of the bicycle tours is covered by a two-page spread which includes a summary of the tour, an elevation graph, a written description, a map, and photographs taken along the route.

Summary Charts

The summary charts tell the reader at a glance the general location of the route, its distance, the amount of traffic, approximate riding time, and a very subjective rating of the route. The riding time is approximate because people bicycle at different speeds. Riding speed is a very personal thing. One 18-year-old nonathletic-looking fellow we met took it upon himself to bicycle from Eugene to the little town of Ontario on the eastern border of the state, averaging over 120 miles per day. And there are the "A" riders in a Portland touring club who mark out a 70-mile route for their Saturday morning ride, planning to maintain a speed of 18-22 mph.

There are other ways of bicycling, too. Our way is to amble along, stopping here and there to smell the flowers, take in the view, shoot a photograph or two. We never travel so fast that we cannot converse with our riding companions — that is one of the wonderful pleasures of bicycling: talking with friends as you pedal along, the noise and congestion of industrial society behind you.

Most people, even out-of-shape beginners, have no difficulty maintaining a riding rate between 7 and 15 mph. If you are going much less than 7 mph, you are liable to topple off your bike simply because you are traveling too slow. And if going much faster than 15 mph, you are probably missing much of the scenery, which is a big part of the reason for a bicycle trip. The approximate riding times for tours in this book are based on a relatively slow, leisurely pace: 8-10 mph. Adjust the given bicycling times to your own rate after you have clocked it.

Assigning ratings to these routes according to difficulty is sticky business. There are no general standards by which to judge difficulty: what may be hard for one person would be a snap for another. Still, there is probably value in these ratings: they give the reader an idea how we, the authors, felt about a particular route. If, after bicycling a few of the suggested tours, you find your judgment differs from ours on the difficulty of the rides, mentally adjust the other ratings accordingly.

Some of the factors which go into these ratings include the number and steepness of hills, the total distance, and the road and traffic conditions.

The ratings are:

    * — an easy ride with no or very few inclines, usually 10 miles or less in length.

    ** — a moderately easy ride with a few more hills, between 15 and 25 miles long.

    *** — a ride of some difficulty, requiring bicyclists to be in reasonably good shape. These routes sometimes have more hills to climb and are always longer, between 25 and 35 miles long.

    **** — the most difficult rides in this book. There are only eight of these rides. All are long (more than 30 miles and up to 60 miles) and most are quite hilly.

Elevation Graphs

A word about the elevation graphs; use them with caution. At first glance it might appear that even the best equipped rock climber couldn't scale some of the inclines — they appear to go straight up. That impression has to do with a distortion in the graphs: the vertical scale (elevation) is in feet, while the horizontal scale (distance biked) is in miles. Hence, the hills seem a lot steeper than they actually are.

Use these graphs as indicators of where inclines are located on a tour and how high they are. After a few times out bicycling, the apparent distortion in the hills will become less worrisome. The graphs will then become a useful tool for evaluating a bike tour.

Maps

The maps accompanying the bike routes are drawn to give sufficient detail for the rider to negotiate his way without problem. Small arrows along the route indicate the preferred riding direction. Of course, the routes can be bicycled in either direction. We recommend, however, that you initially ride in the direction suggested. Save riding the other way for later, until after you have a feeling for the area.

The road to bicycle is easy to distinguish from other roads on the map: it is wider. But this wide line does not mean that the road is wider in reality. Usually the roads forming the bicycle tour are narrower and have much less traffic than the other roads.

A little distortion of necessity crept into some of the maps: a few roads had to be compressed or lengthened for the completed map to fit on the page. So, don't always expect the distances to be proportional to road length indicated on the maps. Use the maps as reliable indicators of road names, intersections, and landmarks you will encounter while bicycling.

The mileage on the map and in the summary chart is only approximate. It may vary a mile or two either way, depending whether you bicycled around the park a few times, backtracked to pick up a dropped glove, or took a detour to see what was at the end of a side street. The mileage is close enough, however, to give you a good idea what kind of distance you are going to cover on a particular tour.

General Information

Bicycles Suitable for Touring

The kind of bike you ride is a very personal thing. Therefore it is difficult to make recommendations to someone considering buying a bike. We will not get involved in those issues here, since many other books describe various bicycle brands and components. Also, people in reputable bike shops know bike brands and components and would gladly help you.

Many tours in this book are within the capability of three-speed bicycle riders, but some tours are simply too hilly for three-speed pleasure. All can be accomplished on inexpensive 10-speeds — those that weigh a little more but cost a lot less, than the very lightweight racing machines. The real joy of bicycling comes in riding a good machine, however, one that is responsive and light, one that sings along the pavement surface, one that shifts to the gear you want when you want. But ride the kind of bike you like, the kind that gives you satisfaction. Forget about fancy equipment, the brand of your derailleur; just enjoy yourself.

Things to Pack for Touring

For some people, the shoes and shorts they are wearing is enough for a bicycle trip. Others pack enough for a four-hour trip that would last ordinary folks a weekend. It all depends on the kind of person you are as to how much you take. We've made a list of some of the things we think are important, and we suggest you use this as a start for making your own list, adding to or subtracting from it as you see fit.

Clothing

For us, weather pretty much determines what we wear. A sweat shirt and perhaps a jacket if it's windy and cold, a t-shirt if it's warm and sunny. A light, brightly-colored, wind-resistant parka is a nice thing to have, both for protection from the wind and for added safety.

Shorts, jeans, and sweat pants all perform satisfactorily. Take your pick. If you are into fashions and the appropriate dress for the appropriate sport, choose special cycling pants.

Ditto for shoes: the cycling elite would not be seen atop their steeds without genuine cycling shoes complete with cleats. But we have found plain, low-cut tennis shoes work fine.

A hat can save your head from sunburn and your body from heat exhaustion. Fit one to size, preferably the kind equipped with a front visor. Gloves can also come in handy, particularly in the cold, wet weather through which Oregonians must suffer. With gloves your fingers will stay warm enough to flex the brake levers on cold rides.

Food

Our idea of a good lunch is a loaf of fine French bread, a liter of Chianti, and some mild Dutch cheese. Add a few friends, a warm summer day, and some natural uncongested surroundings and you have what we consider the ideal bicycling situation. But whether you are into granola, Hershey bars, or some liquid energy formula poured into your special bicycle water bottle, pack a bite to eat. These tours are planned for relaxation and for a lunch or snack break at the midway point. Take advantage of the situation. Live it up a little!

Bicycle Accessories

A number of accessories can make your biking safer and more enjoyable. Some are:

Toe clips: Resembling stirrups, clips strap your feet to the pedals and thereby allow you to benefit from the upward stroke of your legs as well as the downward stroke. Some people estimate that toe clips increase bicycling efficiency by as much as 30 percent. Once you learn how to use them, there is no danger of not being able to remove your feet from the pedals — a fear many beginners have.

Trouser clips: These are springy metal devices that hold your pant legs tight, preventing the material from getting greasy and entangled in the bicycle chain. They are cheap and well worth having. Rubber bands, twine, and brightly-colored yarn also work well.

Bicycle water bottles: Special plastic containers fit onto the frame of the bike and allow the rider to gulp his favorite drink while on the move. They are nice to have on long tours.

A Bicycle Repair kit: This is a must. There is nothing quite so frustrating as a flat tire on a lonely road far from anything. Always carry a tube patch kit, three tire irons (for removing clincher tires from their rims), and a small hand pump, which can be mounted on the bicycle frame. Other tools — such as a crescent wrench, screwdriver, and tire gauge — can be taken along, but are not really necessary. If your bicycle has sew-up tires, carry a spare. Forget about repairing one of these tires on the road; save it until you get home.

Accessory bags: Be they mounted on the handlebars, behind the saddle, on the rear tire carrier, or on the shoulders of the rider, these are good to have. They provide space for storing all the little things you feel like taking on your trip. Check your local bike shops to get an idea of the variety available.

Transporting Bicycles

Many of the tours in this book will be some distance from your home, certainly too far to bicycle in a short time. In these cases we recommend transporting your bike to the starting point of a tour by car. There are many commercially-made bicycle car racks. Some mount bikes on the car roof, some on the rear trunk, some on the rear bumper. It is also possible to make your own car roof rack; plans are available in some of the general interest bike books.

The best place for your bike, however, is inside the car. Here, there is little chance of damage to the bike should someone rear-end your car or should you drive under a very low bridge. If you have quick-release wheels on your bike, it can be disassembled quite easily and transported in the rear seat area. A station wagon can carry two bikes in its storage area.

Bicycle Clubs and Organizations

Bicycle clubs are springing up about as fast as manufacturers are assembling two-wheel vehicles. There are clubs for racing enthusiasts, clubs for Sunday touring, and general interest clubs that try to do everything. The best way to find out what clubs are active in your area is to contact your city's parks and recreation department. Most of the people in these offices keep fairly abreast on bicycling activity.

There are other organizations and committees at work on bicycle-related issues. Many communities have citizen committees which work on safety and placement of bike routes within the city. Check City Hall for information on these committees, too.

Many colleges and universities in the state now offer courses on bicycling — some of which involve touring, bicycle repair, and design of bicycling facilities. Check the course bulletin of your local college or university for more details.

One national organization worth mentioning is the League of American Wheelmen. This organization has been around almost as long as the bicycle and provides its members with a membership list (very useful for cross-country touring) and a monthly newsletter. For information about joining, write to: LAW, c/o Phyllis W. Harmon, 356 Robert Ave., Wheeling, Ill. 60090.

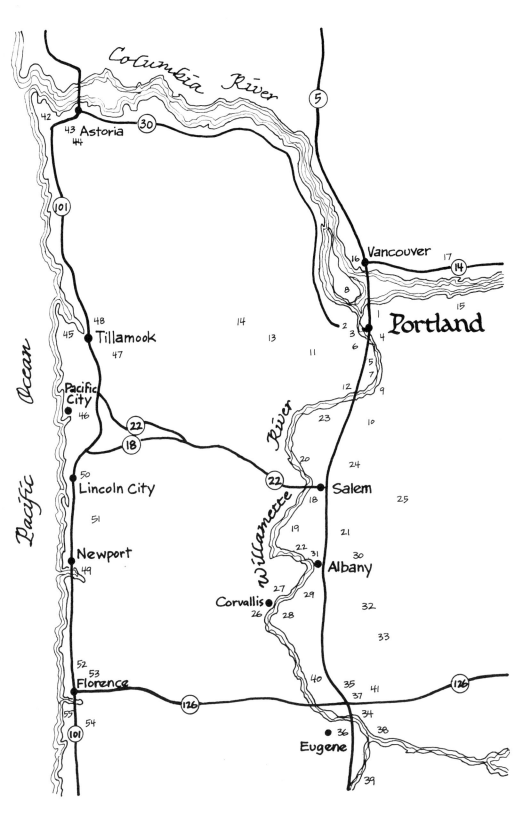

Portland Metropolitan Area

1 MARINE DRIVE ROUTE

General location: Portland, along Columbia River
Distance: 27½ miles round trip
Riding time: 3 hours
Traffic conditions: moderate; may be heavy on weekends
Road conditions: wide shoulder for bicyclists to use
Ride rating: * * *

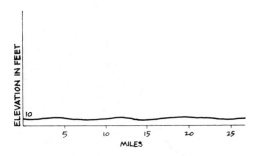

This bike route starts at Delta Park, an expanse of grass and facilities where you can watch anything from a baseball game to kids flying model airplanes to a local rock group performing. It ends at Blue Lake Park, a facility with hundreds of picnic tables and a lake inhabited by scores of mallards, swans, geese and many other kinds of waterfowl. In between we have the mighty Columbia, the Portland sailor's sad equivalent of Seattle's Puget Sound, and the International Airport. Despite the noise and air pollution the monster jets create, there is still a feeling of excitement as they takeoff or lower their flaps to land. You can view it all at very close range along this route.

Begin bicycling northeast from the entrance to Delta Park at the intersection of N. Marine Drive and N. Union Ave. Marine Drive is sometimes rather busy with weekend motorists, but there is a wide shoulder on both sides of the road

bicyclists may use with safety. Along the way are a number of yacht clubs and moorings for houseboats, some of which are very distinctive. On a windy day it's truly impressive to see brightly-colored spinnakers aloft some of the sleek sailing ships which make the Columbia their harbor.

Blue Lake Park is near the end of Marine Drive. Picnic sites and recreation facilities are available for both young and old.

The return trip duplicates the route to Blue Lake, except for a short but very pleasant loop around Blue Lake on Interlachen Lane. It intersects Marine Drive at the eastern-most tip of the lake. This little lane is posted, requesting drivers not to exceed 15 mph. (No speeding, those racers among you!) It soon reunites with Marine Drive. The remainder of the route is along Marine Drive, back to Delta Park.

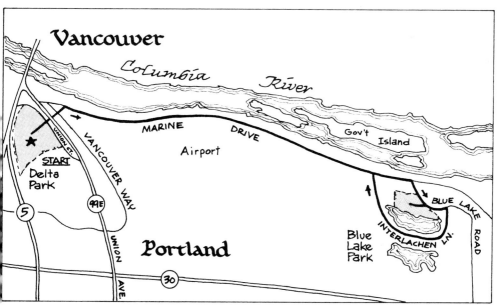

2 WASHINGTON PARK LOOP

General Location: near Central Portland
Distance:
   short loop: 7 miles
   long route: 9½ miles
Riding time: 1 hour
Traffic conditions: light to moderate
Road conditions: short steep inclines
Ride rating:
   short loop: *
   long route: **

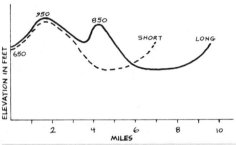

"Let's go to the zoo, zoo, zoo; how about you, you, you . . . ." So goes the children's song, and so go we on this loop laden with exhibits and gardens and special places to see. There's the Portland Zoo, of course, plus Oregon Museum of Science and Industry (OMSI), and the Western Forestry Center — all at the edge of Washington Park. In other parts of the park which the loop passes there are the Pittock Mansion, the Japanese Gardens, the International Rose Test Gardens, and the Lewis and Clark Monument. All this is much more than one can manage to see in a single visit, which is all right because Washington Park is the kind of place a person likes to come back to, to bicycle around, to picnic at, and to just plain enjoy.

There are two versions to the Washington Park loop: one that includes Pittock Mansion and one that does not. Anyone who has driven up to the Mansion in an auto knows the incline awaiting the bicyclist — a climb that will make even the most athletic rider huff and puff. The hills in the short loop are not all that easy either, but they should be manageable by most 10-speed riders.

Begin the loop at the Portland Zoo, just off Highway 26, (S.W. Canyon Road). Turn right onto Portland Scenic Drive which is parallel to Highway 26. At S.W. Skyline Boulevard, an intersection over-

16

run with gas stations, turn right, shifting down to climb the coming hill.

Near the top, Skyline intersects S.W. Fairview; turn right on Fairview and coast downhill. Occasionally through the trees you can get a glimpse of Portland below, sprawling forever and ever. The north entrance to the Zoo is off to the right and, a little farther on the left, is Hoyt Arboretum. Just beyond the picnic grounds near the Arboretum is S.W. Fisher Lane. If you are bound for Pittock Mansion, turn left on Fisher; otherwise continue on Fairview to Kingston Avenue, turning right to reach the tennis courts and Rose Gardens.

To reach the Mansion, follow Fisher along its windy downhill path through the Arboretum until it intersects W. Burnside Road. Turn right on Burnside and ride to the next street on the left, N.W. Barnes Road which you turn onto, following it to N.W. Irving where you walk if you are already tired, to Pittock Mansion. A tour through the Mansion provides some insight into how the super-rich lived at the turn of the century. The view from the 1,000-foot knoll gives a panoramic view of Portland.

To return to Washington Park, coast down to Burnside Road, turn left, and just after a blinking yellow light, turn to the right on Tichner Street. It's a steep climb, but it is short. Turn right on Kingston Avenue and bicycle straight to the Rose Gardens.

This area is a fine place to stop and relax. Plenty of lawn to lay on, flowers to smell, exciting tennis matches to watch. After thoroughly relaxing and exploring the area, follow the Portland Scenic Drive back to the Zoo. Bicycle through the Zoo gates and up a steep hill. Eventually, however, it will go down into the Portland Zoo area. Once back to the starting point, don't miss visiting the Zoo.

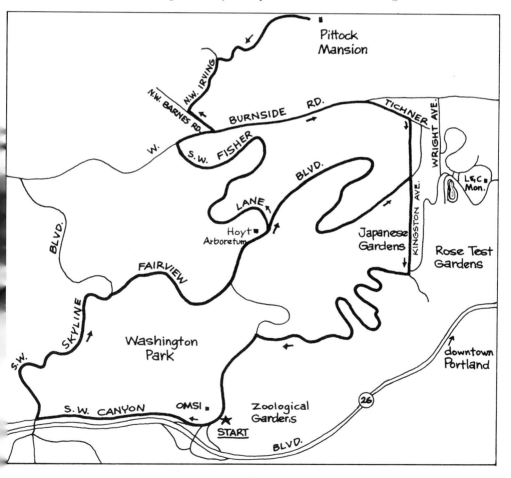

3 COUNCIL CREST PARK LOOP

General location: Central Portland
Distance: 9½ miles
Riding time: 1 hour
Traffic conditions: light
Road conditions: level except for climb to park
Ride rating: *

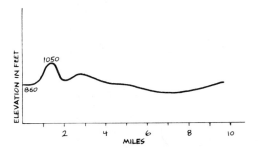

One of the most scenic rides within Portland is this figure eight loop around Council Crest Park. To reach the loop from downtown Portland, drive toward Washington Park on S.W. Canyon Road (U.S. 26). Take the exit just beyond the Portland Zoo, cross the freeway and turn left onto S.W. Humphrey Boulevard. Follow Humphrey to a four-way intersection with a blinking signal. On one corner is a Shell station, on another is St. Thomas Moore Catholic Church, and a stone's throw away is a large parking lot suitable for leaving your car and beginning the bicycle tour.

Bicycle back to the Shell station and turn right on S.W. Talbot. There is a short hill here, one of the few on this loop. At the top is a three-way intersection. The middle route, S.W. Talbot Terrace, takes you up some more hills to Council Crest Park. If your legs are in shape it's worth the climb; on a clear day the view is spectacular: you can see several mountains, including Mt. Rainier, St. Helens, Mt. Hood, and Mt. Jefferson. Their exact location is indicated on a large compass on the top of the knoll. To the west are the valleys harboring Beaverton, Hillsboro, and other suburbs. This grassy park has a few picnic tables, too.

Return to the bicycle loop the same way you came up. On reaching the three-way intersection, turn to the right on S.W. Talbot Road. Follow it through an underpass where you will reach S.W. Fairmount Boulevard. Remain on this windy, tree-lined road until it loops around back to Talbot. There are some impressive homes along the way, and some view points worth stopping at. It's all very quiet and peaceful and beautiful.

At Talbot, return to the blinking signal light, but continue straight rather than turning left to the parking lot and Shell station. Called S.W. Humphrey Boulevard, this quiet road is a little hillier, but most of the inclines are down, not up. Follow Humphrey until it intersects with Scholls Ferry Road and Hewitt Boulevard. Take Hewitt for the last leg of this figure eight tour. Hewitt intersects Patton Road just before the parking lot and the church.

Fountain at Council Crest

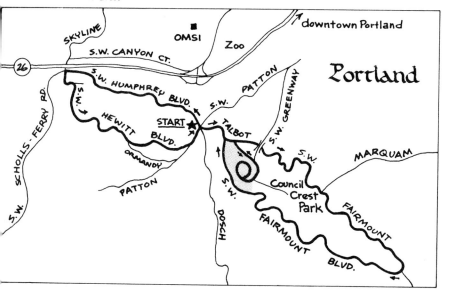

4 REED COLLEGE LOOP

General location: southeast Portland
Distance: 11½ miles
Riding time: 1 hour
Traffic conditions: light to moderate
Road conditions: mainly residential streets
Ride rating: *

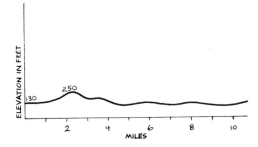

Reed College, one of the most rigorous academic institutions in America, provides the starting point for this bicycle tour which goes through surrounding rural-residential areas, the small suburban town of Milwaukie, and the expansive Westmoreland Park. Reed College is located near the east bank of the Willamette River, about 5 miles from downtown Portland, very near Highway 99E. Rhododendron Test Gardens are near the campus as well as Crystal Springs Lake.

Leave the college through the main gates, bicycling south along Reed College Place. This street is lined with large maple trees, which provide welcome shade in the summertime as you ride past

Westmoreland Park

a number of stately homes.

At the end of Reed College Place, where it intersects S.E. Crystal Springs Boulevard, turn left. Turn left again at S.E. 45th Street. In five blocks, after a short climb, you will reach S.E. Flavel Drive, where you turn right. Trinity United Church is located on the corner of 45th and Flavel.

Follow this road, which after it crosses Johnson Creek Boulevard is called Linwood Avenue, until it merges with Lake Road, just after the second set of railroad tracks and Railroad Avenue. Take Lake Road, a much busier route, into the town of Milwaukie. After passing through the downtown section, turn left on Harrison Street, at the end of 21st Street, across

from the Junior High School. Up ahead is busy McLoughlin Boulevard, which you cross, taking the left-hand fork a block to the north. Follow this road — called River Road and later 17th Street — all the way to S.E. Nehalem Street. Here you can make a right and reach Westmoreland Park.

This park has extensive recreational facilities — plenty of lawn, picnic tables, ponds, and slides and swings for children. It even has a fly casting pool and lawn bowling greens. Definitely a nice place.

Return to Reed College by way of S.E. Bybee Boulevard, crossing Highway 99E and passing the Eastmoreland Golf Course, a public course. At Reed College Place, turn left, to return to the campus.

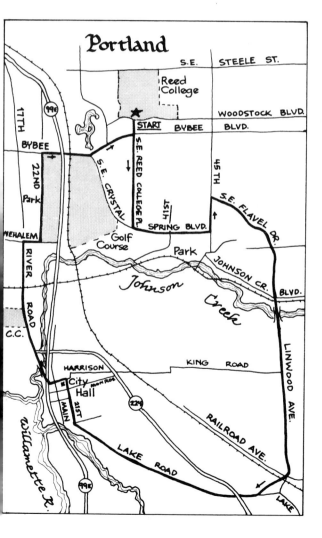

5 LAKE OSWEGO LOOP

General location: south of Portland
Distance: 7 miles
Riding time: ¾ hour
Traffic conditions: light
Road conditions: lakeshore boulevards and
  residential streets
Ride rating: *

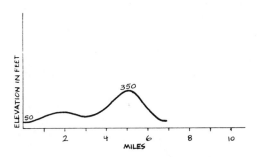

Lake Oswego is an exclusive residential area, situated south of downtown Portland, with a beautiful man-made lake especially developed for the residents of the community. All accesses to the lakefront are restricted to residents having special keys or passes; there are no public parks along the lake. But there is a nice public park along the Willamette River.

The starting point for this short loop is that very park, George Rogers Park, located at the mouth of Lake Oswego and extending to the shores of the Willamette River. In this very pleasant area, complete with picnic facilities, ball field, boat launch, and flower garden, rests the once-active stone chimney of Oregon's first iron foundry. This chimney symbolizes the dream of some earlier settlers to make Oswego the "Pittsburg of the West." Fortunately, for the residents living in the area today, the industry never really got off the ground. The massive chimney remains as a monument to an ambitious but unsuccessful Oregon enterprise.

Leave the park, turn north on State Street and, after one block, turn left at the traffic signal, onto Middlecrest Road. Follow this road to Kenwood and make a right to North Shore Road. Turn left on North Shore Road and cross the bridge separating two parts of the lake. Follow North Shore until just before it dead ends and turn to the right, crossing railroad tracks. At Iron Mountain Boulevard turn left. Bicycle along it to Lake View Boulevard, where you make a left. This road follows the lakefront closely.

Turn off Lake View to the left onto where South Shore Boulevard intersects it. Here you will cross several lake inlets and climb the steepest section of the tour. South Shore eventually merges with McVey Avenue. Bear left on McVey and follow it down to State Street and George Rogers Park.

Lake Oswego

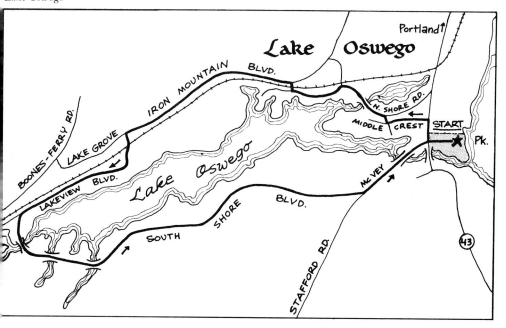

6 LEWIS AND CLARK COLLEGE LOOP

General location: south of downtown Portland
Distance: 10½ miles
Riding time: 1 hour
Traffic conditions: light to moderate
Road conditions: isolated residential and rural roads
Ride rating: **

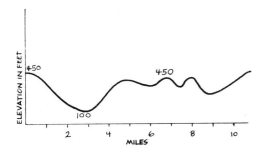

Lewis and Clark College is regarded by authorities as one of the most beautiful college campuses in the country. But even if the wooded, 110-acre site had not achieved national acclaim by those who judge architectural and landscape beauty, Lewis and Clark would still rank high in the opinion of Portlanders and other Oregonians familiar with the campus. Cobblestone lanes connect the stately buildings, some as old as the college. New, very modern architectural styles are also present, but they nicely blend into the groves of trees. It is definitely a beautiful place to visit.

An additional feature to the area is a short, very invigorating bicycle loop that originates at the Lewis and Clark campus. At the entrance to the college begin bicycling south on Riverside Street, located directly across from the main entrance to the campus. Turn right on S.W. Terwilliger Place. In a block this street meets S.W. Terwilliger Boulevard. Take a left and coast all the way down to Lake Oswego.

At the end of Terwilliger, where the busy Highway 43 intersects the route, turn right toward Lake Oswego. At 'B' Street take a right in the direction of the Lake Oswego Information Center (a large sign points the way). After a few blocks this road becomes a shaded, small lane, and is very pleasant. It ends at Tenth Street. To the right is the ultramodern Lutheran Church, on the corner of Tenth and 'C' Street. Go right one block, then left on 'C' until it merges with Country Club Road. This is a complicated intersection, some six streets coming together.

To the right, across from the beginning of Lake Oswego Country Club, is a section of Iron Mountain Boulevard. Bear right on it, and follow its narrow windy path to Atwater Road. Make a left here, continuing on this sometimes hilly road to Knaus Road, taking this road to S.W. 19th Avenue. Turn right. You will soon be intersecting S.W. Boones Ferry Road. Turn right on Boones Ferry and ride to S.W. Stephenson Street (a blinking yellow light marks the intersection) where you turn left.

Leave Stephenson Street at its intersection with S.W. Lancaster Road, turning right. Remain on this pleasant, wooded road until reaching S.W. Maplecrest Drive. Maplecrest makes a switchback and ends just west of the intersection of Boones Ferry and Terwilliger. Bicycle east on Terwilliger to S.W. Palater and back to Lewis and Clark College. There are plenty of signs along here showing the way.

Administration Building, Lewis & Clark College

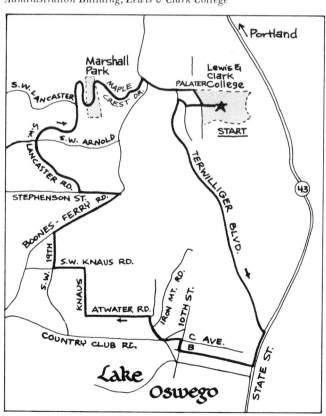

General location: across from Oregon City on Willamette River

Distance:
  short route: 6 miles
  long loop: 13½ miles

Riding time:
  short route: ± ½ hour
  long loop: ± 1½ hours

Traffic conditions: light

Road conditions:
  short route: level and quiet
  long loop: some steep inclines

Ride rating:
  short route: *
  long loop: **

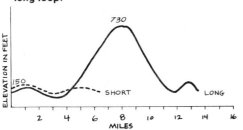

Special Bike Routes are being built around the state at a very rapid rate and sometimes in a very sloppy fashion. But the Bike Routes along the Pacific Highway (Highway 43), connecting Lake Oswego and West Linn, and those in Mary Young Park are very functional and enjoyable to ride. Mary Young Park is a recently opened state facility just north of West Linn which extends from Highway 43 to the shores of the Willamette River. Special bike paths have been constructed in the park, separate from the roads for autos, winding through dense growth.

A nice, short route as well as a longer, hillier loop begin at Mary Young Park. For both versions, leave the park, turning right on the Bike Route along Pacific Highway. In a few hundred yards there is a white guard rail on the right side of the road. A path on the end of it leads to a street which dead ends rather than intersects the highway. This is Old River, a beautiful, quiet road that winds along the Willamette behind Marylhurst College. There are several spots along it where you can view the river.

Old River Drive eventually ends turning into Glenmorrie Drive which winds off to the left of Pacific Highway. At this turning point, there is a footbridge and a path which leads to George Rogers Park in Lake Oswego. Located on county property, this path is slated to be improved for pedestrians and bicyclists.

George Rogers Park marks the turn around point for riders of the short route. To return, simply retrace Old River Drive back to Mary Young Park.

For the long version, leave the park and turn onto McVey Avenue. A green highway sign points in the direction of Wilsonville. This road, which becomes Stafford Road, is mainly uphill. It takes you through residential areas and past a golf course. At the next road on the left, called S.W. Rosemont Road, turn left and follow it up and down its inclines into West Linn. A green highway sign points toward "Rosemont Area" at this intersection.

The road is eventually called Sunset Avenue and goes by the old West Linn City Hall. To return to Mary Young Park, leave the City Hall area by West 'A', where a sign points to "West Linn High School." "A" Street merges with Pacific Highway. From this point the park is a little over a mile away.

Mary Young Park, West Linn

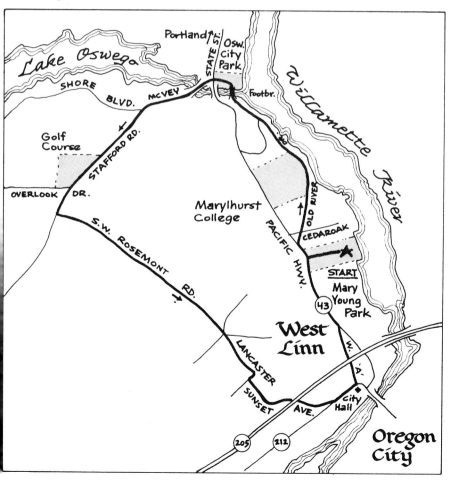

8 SAUVIE ISLAND LOOP

**General location: 12 miles northwest of down-
town Portland on Highway 30**
Distance:
   short loop: 11½ miles
   long loop: 25 miles
Riding time:
   short loop: ±1 hour
   long loop: ±2½ hours
Traffic conditions: nonexistent to light
Road conditions: smooth and level
Ride rating:
   short loop: *
   long loop: **

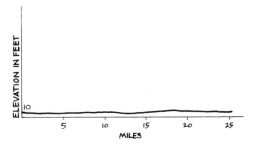

Pastoral beauty of unrivaled quality awaits you on Sauvie Island, only twenty minutes from the heart of Portland. This island, flanked by Oregon's two great rivers, the Willamette and the Columbia, is a paradise for bicyclists. The roads are excellent, the terrain is perfectly flat, the traffic is almost nonexistent, and the surrounding scenery is magnificent.

There is also considerable history associated with the island, well worth investigating and thinking about while peddling around its periphery. The island is named for Laurent Sauvé, a French Canadian who introduced dairy farming to the region back in 1838. Lewis and Clark mentioned the island in their journals. But well before whitemen ex-

plored and settled the island, several Indian nations lived there, fishing salmon from the Columbia and hunting small game in the groves of cottonwood, ash, and oak.

Settlers came to live an isolated, self-contained life on Sauvie, even after the ferry was replaced by the steel bridge in 1950. That sense of isolation remains in large part to this day. It is there for the experiencing.

The best starting point for a tour of the island is at the foot of the single bridge connecting the island with the mainland. There is a large lot used for parking by the many cyclists who come here on weekends. There is also a grocery store nearby, the only store on the island. The loop can be easily bicycled in either direction, since the road is flat and there is seldom wind, but we recommend traveling counter-clockwise (south, away from the grocery store). Bicycling this direction will allow you to stop off at Howell Park for a picnic near the end of the loop.

Branching off the main loop around the island are three roads, all worth exploring. The most westerly one, Sauvie Island Road, follows along the Multnomah Channel, passing the site of Fort Williams, one of the first settlements on the island. Further along is a fleet of houseboats, some of rather impressive architecture. There are also discarded booms in the slough — floats of logs destined for lumber mills, but for some unknown reason never to leave their mooring. This road is 6½ miles long.

To the east of Sauvie Island Road is another route branching off. Called Oak Island Road, it heads in the direction of Sturgeon Lake and the Game Management Area. This diversion is the least interesting of the three; it is three miles long.

Finally, there is Reeder Road, the option offering the most enjoyment. This road follows along the Columbia River and an inlet lined with both weather-worn fishing boats and modern fiberglass sailing yachts. Just over the dike separating road from river there are fine, sandy beaches, great for swimming or fishing. After spending only a little time on this stretch of beach you're bound to see a tug slowly but persistently chugging upstream, towing a barge-load of material to Portland.

On the last leg of the main loop is located the Bybee-Howell House, a registered National Landmark. This plain, nine-room dwelling was one of the first settlements on the island and has been restored and refurbished by volunteers from the Oregon Historical Society. One of the interesting features of the house is that the plaster for the interior had to be shipped around Cape Horn; no plaster was available locally back in the 1850's. The house is located on an 130-acre park, complete with picnic tables nestled in a recently planted fruit orchard. The orchard itself is historical, also, for it has been planted from clippings from famous trees and orchards in Oregon Country. The starting point, grocery store and bridge are less than a mile down the road.

Sauvie Island

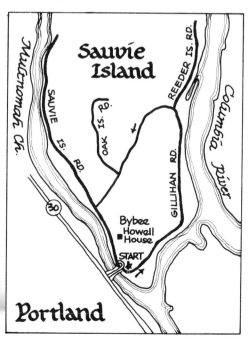

Sauvie Island

9 CLACKAMAS RIVER DRIVE LOOP

General Location: Oregon City
Distance:
  short route: 16 miles
  long loop: 18 miles
Riding time:
  short route: ±1½ hours
  long loop: ±2 hours
Traffic conditions: light to moderate
Road conditions: nearly level along river; hilly thereafter
Ride rating:
  short route: *
  long loop: **

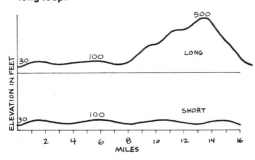

Clackamas River Drive is one of Oregon's most scenic riverbed roads. In the late spring and summer, branches arch over this windy, seldom-traveled lane, providing a cover of beautiful green foliage. An occasional break in the shrubery offers a view of the Clackamas River, slowly making its way to the Willamette.

Start this tour at Kelly Field on the north side of Oregon City. Kelly Field is very near Interstate 205, and one block away from the intersection of Washington Street and Abernathy Road. Leave the field and turn left on Seventeenth Street, heading east. There is a sign indicating Redland and Fishers Mill in that direction.

At a fork in the road, take the route on the left, in the direction of Holcomb Road and Clackamas Heights. It is here that you will encounter your first incline. At the top of the hill turn left on N.E. Apperson Boulevard. Follow this quiet, residential road to its end at a T-crossing with Forsythe Road. To the left, a block away, is Clackamas River Drive. Turn to the right on the drive and begin to enjoy yourself. The road is relatively flat and the traffic is not particularly heavy except on holidays.

Approximately 7 miles from the start is the townsite of Carver, where there is a bridge crossing the river and a small tavern. Just up the road about a ½ mile is a private park (there is an admission fee) which offers facilities for picnicking and swimming. For the short version of this tour, return to the starting point by retracing the route along Clackamas Drive.

For the long version, leave the park, returning to the intersection at the bottom of the incline, just before the bridge. Turn left, in the direction of Redland. At the top of the incline is an intersection, with Baker's Cabin on the right-hand corner. Horace Baker lived here over a century ago and initiated a ferry service across the Clackamas River in the vicinity of the present bridge.

The road to the right of the intersection is nice and isolated, but quite hilly. We recommend bearing left, continuing in the direction of Redland. A short way up this road is a museum of dolls. Over 1,000 dolls of several nationalities and ages are on display in the barn-like museum. The very pleasant elderly lady who runs the museum has written a book on doll repair and intends to establish a

doll hospital. The museum is open to the public and is free of charge.

Redland lies at the end of this quiet road. Turn right at the intersection, this time in the direction of Oregon City. This road is wide and sometimes busy, but it is a speedy and pleasant descent into Oregon City and the starting point, Kelly Field.

Clankamas River

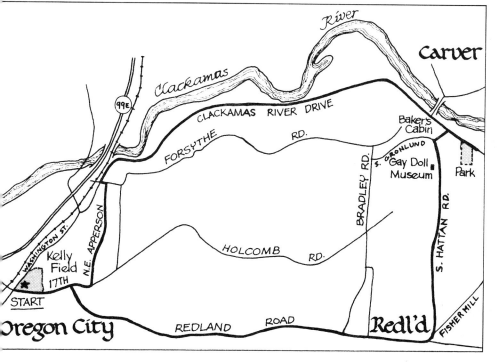

**General location: 7 miles south of Oregon City
on Highway 99E**
Distance:
  short loop: 19½ miles
  long loop: 28½ miles
Riding time:
  short loop: ± 2 hours
  long loop: ± 3 hours
Traffic conditions: light
Road conditions: flat
Ride rating:
  short loop: **
  long loop: ***

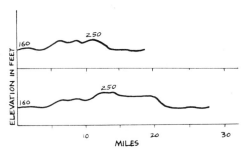

Totem Pole Near Wagon Wheel Park

Some bicycle tours may seem like they have little to offer in terms of local history or well-known tourist sites. But such tours usually make up for these "defects" through a plentitude of leisurely, scenic cycling country. This tour, located between Canby and Mulino, has lots of that: flat farmland, few cars, and a very pleasant park along the Molalla River.

Canby is located on Highway 99E, about 8½ miles south of Oregon City, near the Willamette River. Start this tour at the intersection of 99E and Ivy Street. Bicycle south on Ivy, crossing the Molalla River, until coming to an intersection with a sign indicating Macksburg to the left. Turn left, passing through the Macksburg townsite, and continue on toward Liberal, another small village, this one being named after a similar town in Missouri which is reputed to have had easy credit.

At Liberal, persons bicycling the short loop version should turn left on Highway 213. About a half-mile up the road on the right is Wagon Wheel Park, just before a bridge crossing the Molalla

River. There is a golf course across from the park on the left, and a totem pole standing in the parking lot. To return to the starting point, follow the long loop version from this park.

For those bicycling the long version of this tour, continue straight at Liberal, crossing Highway 213 onto Wiles Road. Remain on Wiles Road until reaching Highway 211, where you turn left and cross the river.

At the next intersection, the one with the Meadowbrook Grocery Store on the corner, turn left in the direction of Union Mills and Mulino. Union Mills, now not much more than a name along the road, used to sport a sawmill, wool carding machinery, and a planing mill — all good reasons for calling the locality by its present name. At the intersection with Highway 213, turn left, cross the river, and relax at Wagon Wheel Park.

To return to Canby, head north along Highway 213 toward Mulino. In about 1½ miles is an intersection with the road to the left marked by a sign indicating Canby and "Post Office."

Follow this road and the signs to Canby. Turn left just before an old railroad truss bridge onto Mundorf Road. At the intersection ahead with a swimming pool and a school, turn right, following this road for the remaining mile to Canby and the starting point.

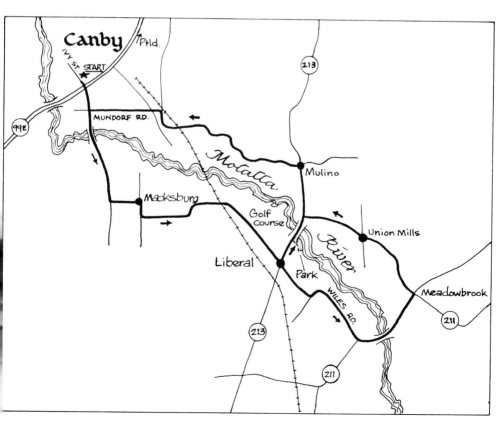

Canby

Ptld.

IVY ST. START

213

99E

MUNDORF RD.

Molalla

Mulino

Macksburg

Golf Course

River

Union Mills

Liberal

Park

WILES RD.

Meadowbrook

213

211

211

General location: west of Portland along Highway 8

Distance:
short loop: 10½ miles
long loop: 16 miles

Riding time:
short loop: ± 1 hour
long loop: ± 1½ hours

Traffic conditions: light to moderate

Road conditions: flat

Ride rating:
short loop: *
long loop: **

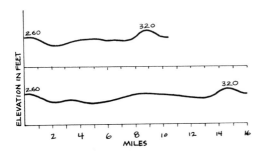

There's something very nice and convenient about hopping on your bike at your house, cycling a good, auto-free loop, one with plenty of rolling farmland; and returning a few hours later to do whatever else you planned for the day. This ideal is reality for people living in the Beaverton area for there are many secondary roads branching off from the suburban center, roads with little traffic and lots of farmland.

To reach the starting point of this loop from downtown Portland, take Sunset Highway (Highway 26) east to the S.W. Cedar Hills Boulevard turnoff. Drive south to Cedar Hills Park, at the northern tip of the Beaverton city limits.

Begin bicycling from this park south on Cedar Hills Boulevard to the first intersection, which is with S.W. Walker Road. Turn right and follow this road through housing developments that become fewer and fewer the farther you bicycle. The Oregon Graduate Center, built in the early '60s, is off to the left.

For the short version of this loop, turn to the right at N.W. Cornell Road. Bicycle back to the community of Cedar Mill on this road, crossing Highway 26 and joining the long version of the loop.

To bicycle the long version, continue west on Walker Road to Cornelius Pass Road. Turn right, heading north to West Union. There is a sizeable power station on the right. At West Union Road, turn right and cycle past open farmland all the way to N.W. 143rd Avenue. Here you turn right again to N.W. Cornell Road, merging with the short loop version. Sunset High School is situated on the corner, a multicolored mural clearly visible on one of its buildings.

Proceed toward Cedar Hills, turning right at N.W. Barnes Road. This road takes you back to Sunset Highway, under it, and onto S.W. Cedar Hills Boulevard. Cedar Hills Park is just ahead.

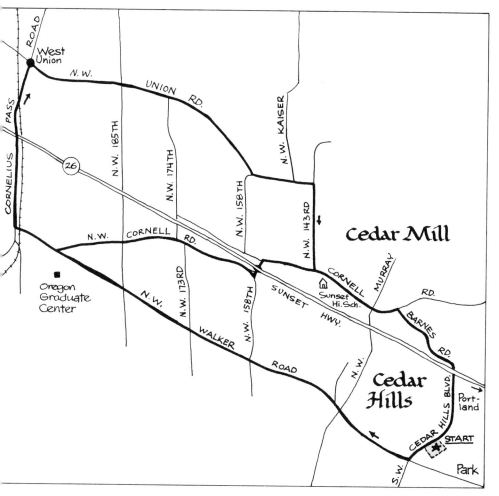

12 NEWBERG-CANBY FERRY LOOP

General location: 23 miles south of Portland along Highway 99W
Distance:
  short loop: 30 miles
  long loop: 43½ miles
Riding time:
  short loop: ± 3 hours
  long loop: ± 4 hours
Traffic conditions: light to moderate
Road conditions: mostly level; some hills
Ride rating:
  short loop: ***
  long loop: ****

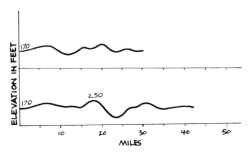

In many ways, the beginning and end of this loop are the nicest parts. Not to say that the filbert orchards, the views of the Willamette, the narrow tree-lined lanes, and the ride on the Canby Ferry are insignificant. Just that Herbert Hoover Park in Newberg is a nice sunken refuge — a perfect place from which to begin and to return.

Hoover Park is located on U.S. 99W, just west of the merger of Highways 219 and 99W, and just across the street from the sign pointing to George Fox College, a small Quaker school on the hill.

To begin the loop, head east on Oregon 219, the Hillsboro-Silverton Highway, past the Sportsman Airpark, to the Wilsonville Road, where you turn left, heading east again. Follow this road all the way into Wilsonville, about 13 miles. Here, at the intersection with Interstate 5, you must make the decision to do the long or short version of the loop. For the short version, climb the southbound freeway ramp and cross the Willamette. This is the only section of any loop in the book that requires bicycling on a freeway. It is the only way to cross the river here. But the section is short — less than a mile — and the freeway shoulder is exceptionally wide. It is perfectly legal for bicyclists to ride this part of Interstate 5; moreover it is safe, probably safer than the typical city artery during rush hour. (Bicycles may legally use all freeways in the state except some around Portland and Eugene.) Still, exercise caution; keep well to the right of the traffic lanes.

Once across the river take the first exit and bicycle toward Champoeg State Park, following the instructions given below for this same stretch on the long version.

For the long version, bicycle under the freeway, past a golf course, to Mountain Road. Turn right here, in the direction of the Canby Ferry sign. Continue straight until the road ends; then turn right, toward the ferry, which is located at the end of this road. Cross the river to Canby.

Canby is one of Oregon's horticultural centers, evident by the orchards of holly and fields of dahlias and other flowers grown for bulbs and seed. There is a small park along the road into town if you want to stop and relax. ("No Bicycling" signs are very prominently displayed in the park!) If you want to go further and explore the downtown sites, continue on, but you must eventually retrace your tracks to Knight Bridge Road on the north side of Canby in order to follow the rest of the loop.

Turn right on Knight Bridge Road and follow it to Knight's Bridge which spans the Molalla River, and then to Red Bridge, near a private park. Continue bicycling west until you pass under Interstate 5. Immediately afterwards is a small road that parallels this freeway. Turn right heading north. It will take you back to the Willamette River to the place riders of the short version ended up after crossing the river on the freeway.

Turn left, bicycling west, passing a boat launching operation. Pass through Butteville, taking time out to chat with the 81-year-old lady who runs the general store and knows other people around the area that are "older than God."

Once out of Butteville, head toward Champoeg State Park. This is another "must" stop. A lot of Oregon history took place here; a lot of it is well-preserved in both the Newell House Museum and the Pioneer Cabin within the park. Read the Champoeg Loop description in the Willamette Valley section for more information on the park.

From Champoeg, continue bicycling east until you reach Oregon 219, where you turn right and head north to Newberg. Turn off Oregon 219 just beyond the airport, to the left. Follow 2nd Street straight into Hoover Park.

Farmland near Newberg

37

General location: west of Portland along Highway 8
Distance:
  short loop: 20 miles
  long loop: 28½ miles
Riding time:
  short loop: ±2 hours
  long loop: ±3 hours
Traffic conditions: light
Road conditions: few hills; some long straight sections
Ride rating:
  short loop: **
  long loop: ***

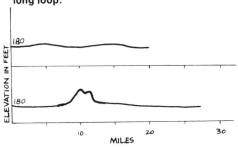

One of Oregon's oldest and most beautiful churches is situated along this countryside loop. The "Old Scotch Church," dedicated in 1878, is of simple, white board construction, its eight-sided steeple and gothic stained glass windows creating a striking appearance. The founders of the church all came from Glasgow, Scotland, and settled on these Tualatin Plains. Many of them are buried in the nearby cemetery, along with prominent Oregon mountainmen such as Joe Meek.

Begin this loop at Shute Park in Hillsboro along the Tualatin Valley Highway (Oregon 8) at the intersection with Maple Street, across from the city swimming pool and roller rink. Bicycle southeast on Highway 8 for one-half mile to S.E. River Road, where you turn right. Follow this road to S.E. Grabel Road and turn right again, heading toward Forest Hills Golf Course.

At the intersection with Oregon 219, turn right and then, shortly, left, always following the signs to Forest Hills Golf Course. Some 7 miles from the start is the golf clubhouse and an intersection with Golf Course Road. Turn right in the direction of Blooming, which you'll reach in a matter of minutes. Here, at Blooming, is the intersection of decision: the short or the long version. For the short version, continue straight on Golf Course Road, passing through Cornelius and crossing Oregon 8. Keep pedalling straight ahead until intersecting Verboort Road, where the long and short versions merge, and where you turn to the right.

For the long loop, turn left on the Blooming-Fernhill Road, following it up and down the hills between Blooming and Fernhill. This road eventually merges with Fernhill Road, which you turn onto and follow into Forest Grove. Turn left on Highway 8 and proceed to Pacific University.

Leave the University via Sunset Drive (Oregon 47) and remain on it until reaching Purdin Road, the turnoff for Verboort, the site of the popular sausage festival each fall.

Old Scotch Church

Almost 18 miles from the beginning of this loop you will intersect Cornelius-Schefflin Road, the point where the short and long versions merge, and where you bear to the left. Pass the Zion Church and cross Glencoe Road, continuing straight toward the Old Scotch Church — another nice place to stop.

From the church, turn right on Jackson Road and head south, back into Hillsboro. At N.W. Evergreen, turn right to reconnect with N.W. Jackson School Road. Follow it until reaching N.E. 5th, taking it to Walnut, and then turning left to Shute Park.

Near Forest Grove

14 FOREST GROVE LOOP

**General location: 24 miles west of Portland
along Highway 8**
Distance: 19 miles
Riding time: ±2 hours
Traffic conditions: light
Road conditions: short section of gravel
Ride rating: **

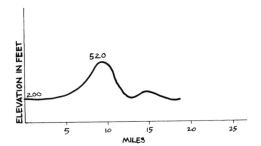

Semirural living, in the way that it is practiced in and around Forest Grove, has an attraction not found in many other places. There is Pacific University, a center of academic and cultural life, in the town of Forest Grove. But no more than a football field away one can watch farmers plow their fields or tend their orchards. Forest Grove is definitely a small town, but without the usually associated provincialism. This tour provides a flavor of both the town and the surrounding region.

Begin bicycling at Pacific University in Forest Grove (24 miles west of Portland on Oregon 8), at the intersection of College Way and University Avenue. Head west, jogging over to 23rd Avenue after one block. Take Gales Way, which angles to the right. At another fork a few blocks later, bear right toward the townsite of Thatcher on Thatcher Road. There is yet another fork four miles from town; turn left again toward Thatcher.

Remain on Hillside Road, past farms and orchards, and eventually up an incline. At the top is Hillside Cemetery, founded in 1887, and the ancient oaks on the corner provide a shaded resting place.

Hillside Road ends at the cemetery, intersecting Clapshaw Road. Turn left on Clapshaw and climb another hill, the last of the major exertions on this loop. On the downward side there is a section which is gravel and requires careful bicycling. Travel slowly here, for the sake of your tires and your shins.

Balm Grove Park is a short way to the right at the next intersection. This park, however, is private; an entrance fee must be paid to use the picnic facilities and to wade in the creek. To the left at the intersection, also only a short distance, is Gales Creek junction which sports a grocery store and a tavern.

Whatever your choice — park, store, or tavern — you must eventually head south along that road, Highway 8. Although labeled a highway, the traffic is very light and is no major impediment to enjoying the countryside.

Leave Highway 8 at Springtown Road, turning right at the road sign saying "Dilley 5 miles." At the next intersection, after about 3 miles, turn left and head back to Forest Grove, following the streets indicated on the map, and to Pacific University.

15 SANDY RIVER LOOP

General location: east of Portland near Trout-dale
Distance:
   short route: 13 miles
   long loop: 32 miles
Riding time:
   short route: ±1½ hours
   long loop: ±3 hours
Traffic conditions: light
Road conditions: curvy, steep climbs
Ride rating:
   short route: *
   long loop: **

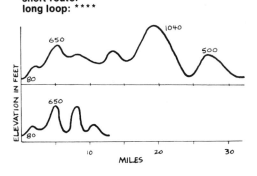

This bike tour has the most hills to climb and is perhaps the most difficult, although not the longest, trail in the book. It is not, however, an impossible trek. Both Elske and I bicycled it, and we're not star athletes. But Elske ended up walking most of the inclines. So, if you are in moderate shape and don't mind combining a little hiking with your bicycling, try this tour. The scenic rewards are great indeed. And the parks along the Sandy River — Dabney at the start, Oxbow a few miles away, and Dodge Park at the halfway point — are some of the best in the state.

To reach the starting point, Dabney State Park, drive east of Portland on Interstate 80 and take the Lewis and Clark State Park turnoff. Pass by Lewis and Clark Park, remaining on the east side of Sandy River, and drive south following the river for approximately three miles to Dabney. An alternate route

from Portland is to drive east on Stark Street to the park.

At Dabney, mount your two-wheeler, leave the park, turn left at the entrance, and cross the bridge a few hundred yards north of the park. Climb the first of many hills on S.E. Stark, turning off to the left about a mile from the park. This turn is almost a 180 degree switchback onto Kerslake Road. Remain on this road until reaching S.E. Division Street, about 2½ miles from the park.

Follow Division to the intersection with Hosner Road and the turnoff to Oxbow Park. The road down to Oxbow and the river is very steep and should be cycled with care. The park is a good stopping and turn-around point for riders not interested in the long loop.

For riders continuing on to Dodge Park, turn right on S.E. Hosner Road. Hosner dead-ends at S.E. Lusted, where you turn left. This road becomes Herrick Road and soon it begins a steep descent into the Sandy River canyon — a speedy swoop downward! At the bottom, across a bridge, is Dodge Park. Stop, relax, take a swim, enjoy yourself.

If you thought the earlier hills were pretty tame stuff, the ones coming may be more to your liking. Leave Dodge and the swimming hole, going past the corner grocery store, and up the windy, steep two-lane road. At the top, two miles later, you'll come to a three-way intersection; turn left toward Bull Run as indicated on the sign. Off to the left you'll soon see an airport, of all things, nestled away in these primitive backwoods. And if you are inquisitive enough, you'll climb the embankment on the right and discover . . . yes, a lake! Straight ahead, jutting up between the flanking Douglas fir is, of course, that ever present, ever magnificent Mt. Hood.

There is a nice, eye-watering descent ahead, which ends at the bottom of the Bull Run River canyon — amazing how water etched its way through that solid rock. Then yet another climb — shift into your alpine low sprocket for this one.

Another descent and another climb and then you're on top of the world, nearly. Have a look backwards for a view of beautiful Sandy River canyon. The remainder of the trip — all 3½ miles of it — is downhill, through Springdale and into Dabney State Park.

Sandy River

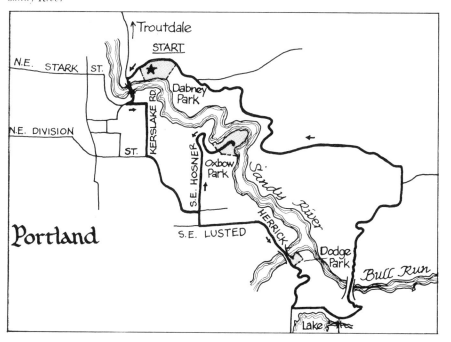

16 VANCOUVER LAKE ROUTE

General location: Vancouver, Wash.
Distance:
  short route: 12 miles
  long route: 26½ miles
Riding time:
  short route: ±1½ hours
  long route: ±2½ hours
Traffic conditions: light
Road conditions: level
**Ride rating: **

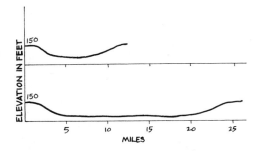

One of the nice things about Portland is the easy access residents have to natural, uncongested surroundings. And one of the escape routes to these surroundings is north, into the city across the Columbia River: Vancouver, Washington. There is a very pleasant, easy-to-ride bike route that follows the Columbia River bed across from the Sauvie Island area.

The starting point is George Marshall Community Center, located adjacent to Interstate 5. When coming from Portland, take the second exit onto Mill Plain Road, turn left at the first street — Fort Vancouver Way — and left again at the next street, McLoughlin Boulevard. The park and center are straight ahead on the left.

Bicycle west on McLoughlin, through the downtown sector of Vancouver, into the residential district, all the way to Lincoln Avenue, where you turn right. At Fourth Plain Boulevard turn left. This road eventually takes on the name Lower River Road and passes some industrial concerns. The farther you pedal on this road, the more isolated it becomes. Soon, it is a rare — almost welcomed — occurrence when a car comes by. (The road eventually dead-ends.)

For the short route, return to Vancouver via the old version of Lower River Road, a short loop in the road which parallels the newer road and ends near an aluminum plant.

For the long route continue bicycling along the only road around. Some parts of it are pretty rough — packed dirt and gravel. But along the way is some beautifully flat grazing land, the narrow road situated along the top of a dike separating the Columbia waters from the farmland. Occasional harbors dot this section of the river, as well as ever-drifting sand dunes — such a joy to climb!

The road ends, appropriately enough at a dairy farm, the silo and barn serving as indicators of the termination of pavement.

The return is along the road already traveled, but seen from an entirely new perspective. It's a different trip.

Near Vancouver Lake

General location: Camas, Washington
Distance:
  short loop: 9¾ miles
  long loop: 23¾ miles
Riding time:
  short loop: ± 1 hour
  long loop: ± 2 hours
Traffic conditions: light
Road conditions: a few hills on both routes
Ride rating:
  short loop: *
  long loop: **

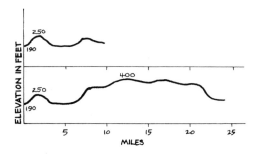

Camas, Washington, may be known to some people for its smoke-billowing paper mill, but for bicyclists there is yet another claim-to-fame for this little town: a very easy, scenic loop which originates at Lacamas Park. This park is a large wooded site complete with boat rentals, swimming and fishing facilities, and picnic grounds. As with many loops in this book, there is both a short and a long version, one for the beginning rider and one for the more aggressive, distance-seeking cyclist.

Camas is approximately 22 miles from downtown Portland. Head north on Interstate 5 to Vancouver and take the first exit onto Highway 14 — the Lewis and Clark Boulevard. Drive east for about 13 miles until reaching the Camas exit. Lacamas Park is located on the north side of town on Highway 500. Signs mark the route of Highway 500.

Begin bicycling around the south shore of Lacamas Lake, on S.E. Lake Road, going past boat rentals and a marshy swamp called "Dead Lake." After some climbs and some nice level cycling, turn right at the intersection with L.D. Strunk Road. Make yet another right at Country Road 116. Lechtenberg Park, a private site located along Lacamas Creek, is just ahead.

Farther on, at County Road 124, you must decide whether you are going to bicycle the short or long version of the tour. For the short version, turn right, and in less than a mile make another right which will take you to the north shore of Lacamas Lake.

For the long version, turn left on County Road 124 in the direction of Proebstel. There is some magnificent farmland along here. Make a left on N.E. Fourth Plains Road, still heading toward Proebstel. Just after the little settlement of Proebstel, across a small bridge, turn right on N.E. 182 toward Camp Bonneville. Follow this road around a left bend until you come to N.E. Ward and a stop sign. Turn right. In a little more than a mile, make another right on N.E. Davis.

This road eventually becomes N.E. 109th and crosses N.E. 212th. At N.E. 222nd, turn right (109th dead ends after a short distance). Follow 222nd to N.E. 83rd where you make a right. At N.E. 217th, a sign indicates Camas is 10 miles to the left. Follow this and the subsequent signs in the direction of Camas.

At County Road 116, however, turn right, in the direction of Lacamas Lake, away from Camas. In a half mile you will come to the intersection with the short bike tour, County Road 126. Turn left and soon you will once again view beautiful Lacamas Lake. At the final intersection bear right and coast down the short hill to the starting point, Lacamas Park.

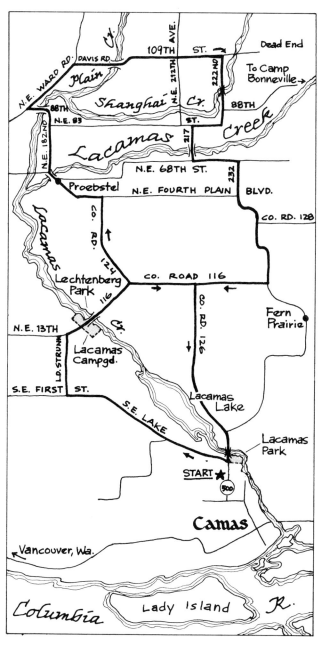

Willamette Valley

18 SALEM BIKE TRAIL

General location: central Salem
Distance: 9 miles
Riding time: ± 1 hour
Traffic conditions: nonexistent to light
Road conditions: level, some places with packed gravel
Ride rating: *

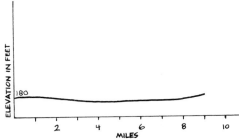

This loop is intentionally short, designed especially for riders who only want to make a brief trip or for people just beginning to experience the thrills of bicycle touring.

Start at the Capitol Park, just west of the Capitol Building, and across the street from Willamette University. Bicycle south on Winter Street for seven blocks until you reach Bush Pasture Park. Bike around the park onto High Street, turning left until reaching Bush Street, where you turn right. Make yet another left turn after passing two main arteries, Liberty and Commercial.

At Owens Street, turn right and follow it around a left bend. Remain on Owens (which soon becomes called River Road South) until you see the green sign

Salem Bike Trail

"Marion County Bicycle Paths" on the right at a road intersection. Turn to the right here and you are on your way to Salem's first especially-designed bicycle trail.

The actual trail — the section which prohibits automobile traffic — is only about 1½ miles long. Still, it's pleasant to ride and view the Willamette River snaking along parts of the path. There are also a number of gravel offshoots that you can explore if you don't mind bicycling on rough surfaces.

The trail terminates at the entrance to the Salem dumps. Don't let this put you off taking the trail, however, or to continuing back on Brown Island Road. There is a beautiful section of road along here which far overshadows any esthetic uneasiness you might have. The road winds through a grove of maple trees, their branches hanging over it.

Follow Brown Island Road until it intersects River Road, where you turn left and head back to town. You might consider stopping off at Bush Pasture Park on your return trip. The 100-acre park has a multitude of paths one can bicycle, as well as picnic facilities, wooded sections, museums, and an art center.

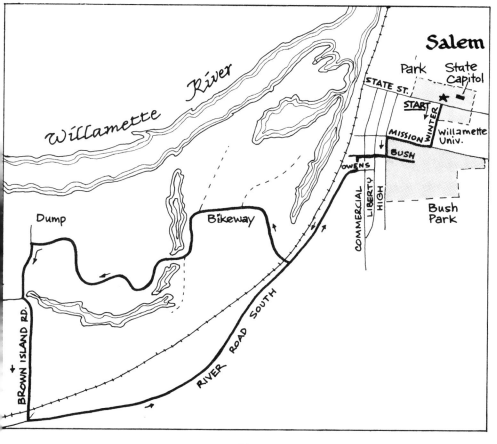

19　SALEM-MONMOUTH ROUTE

General location: Salem area
Distance: 28 miles
Riding time: ±3 hours
Traffic conditions: light
Road conditions: mostly level
Ride rating: ★★

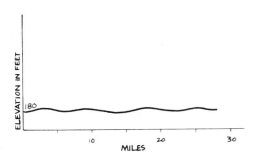

with blackberries and wild shrubs. It also goes through the little town of Independence, its old bank building refurbished and still in use. Another nice point about this route is that bicyclists from either Salem or Monmouth can enjoy it, since it can be started at either end. The following instructions, however, assume point of origin to be Salem.

Start at Bush Pasture Park. If you have not taken the time to explore Bush House, the Art Barn, and the almost 100-acres of park area, you might consider doing so now. It is well worth your time. Leave Bush Park by the exit from Bush House, crossing the main arteries and then turning left to reach Owens Street. Turn right on Owens. Take this street four blocks to its end, where it turns off to the left and becomes River Road. Follow this road all the way into Independence, past the Salem Golf Club, past Roberts Elementary, past old barns and farm houses, past groves of filberts and rows and rows of corn. The only incline of significance is the bridge over the Willamette, and that one poses no bicycling problem. It does provide a fine view of the Willamette, though.

Once over the bridge, turn right toward Independence. In a few blocks you will pass through the heart of this old river town, christened after its namesake in Missouri. Continue straight on Main Street until reaching the City Park, a good place to rest before bicycling on to Monmouth. This park, located along the river, has picnic sites and lush green grass that invites relaxation.

Proceed on to Monmouth by backtracking a few blocks to the intersection with Oregon 51. Turn right, following the sign to Monmouth. Much of this route has a bicycle lane, some of which is separated from the highway.

In Monmouth, bicycle on another Main Street up to Monmouth Avenue, where you turn right to reach Oregon College of Education. This college was founded more than 100 years ago by settlers from Illinois who came West for the very purpose of establishing a Christian college. (It has since become a state-supported school.) The campus has diverse architecture: from modern glass and concrete structures to the original brick college building, Campbell Hall.

Return to Salem by the same route.

Wondering what to do with your sunny summer afternoon? Thinking you might be interested in a bicycle ride if not too long nor too hilly, if it provided some pleasant scenery and uncongested riding? Well, then, this is the tour.

Connecting Salem and Monmouth, this ride covers some beautiful river-bed farmland and skirts hillsides overgrown

Monmouth Bike Route

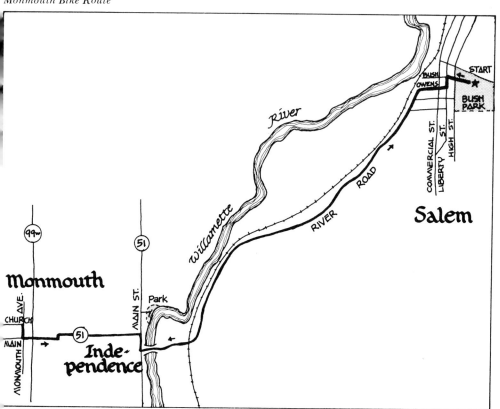

General location: Salem area
Distance: 31 miles
Riding time: ± 3 hours
Traffic conditions: light to moderate
Road conditions: some hills, but mostly level
Ride rating: **

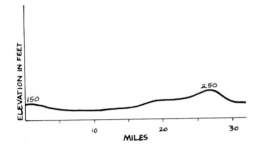

There are only three places left along the Willamette River where ferries transport traffic across the river. One of them is along this bicycle tour, and the tour is worth taking just for that single ebbing experience. But if riding ferry boats is old hat to you, there is much more to entice you to bicycle this 31 mile loop.

Starting at Capitol Park, adjacent to the Capitol Building and across the street from Willamette University, head north on Winter Street. Remain on Winter past Market Street and Fairgrounds Road until it merges with Laurel Avenue. Follow Laurel until it ends at the School for the Deaf, where you turn right and intersect Cherry Avenue. Take Cherry north until it merges with River Road and Cummings Lane at a stop light intersection. Bicycle west on Cummings for a few blocks until reaching Shore Line Drive.

Here you turn to the right and are about to enter orchards and pastures and never-ending fields of hops. This road, which eventually takes on the name Windsor Island Road, is an amazingly isolated farm road looping through some of the richest soil in the valley.

The road eventually ends, however, climbing an escarpment and intersecting Wheatland Road. Turn left and follow Wheatland all the way to the ferry. If you are thirsty or hungry, you will find several well-stocked fruit stands along the way. One of them is owned and run by Paul Townsend, a 70-year-old native to the region. Clad in striped overalls and work boots, Mr. Townsend has been tilling the land here all of his life, and his father did the same a century earlier. Paul Townsend makes great apple juice, recalls riding to Salem on horseback and remembers when electricity first came to the area, and when neighbors used to know and call each other by first names.

If, by the time you reach Wheatland Ferry, you are feeling a little tired and ready for a break, cross on the ferry and press on for less than a mile more and you will reach Maud Williamson State Park, a lovely, wooded park equipped with facilities for picnicking. It's a beautiful spot, one you will want to come back to and enjoy again.

The remainder of the route is all southbound, back to Salem. Take extra caution crossing the bridge from West Salem into downtown Salem. Bicyclists are urged to pedal on the pedestrian walkway, but they should extend the right-of-way to those on foot. From the bridge, simply proceed east on Center Street until reaching Summer Street, one block past Winter. To the right you will see the Capitol Building and your starting point.

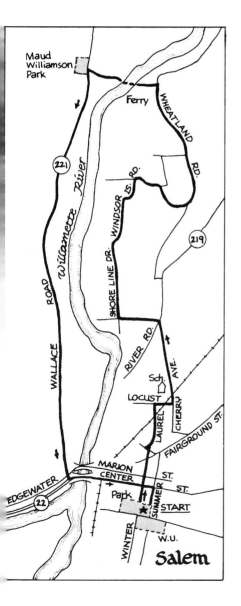

Maud Williamson Park

21 ENCHANTED FOREST LOOP

General location: Salem area
Distance:
  short loop: 22 miles
  long loop: 30½ miles
Riding time:
  short loop: ±2 hours
  long loop: ±3 hours
Traffic conditions: light to moderate
Road conditions: a few hills
Ride rating:
  short loop: **
  long loop: ***

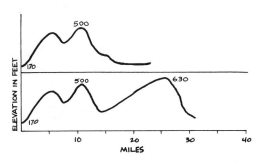

They are all there — Snow White, the Seven Dwarfs, Alice, Humpty Dumpty — all of those childhood friends, and many more. They can be found at the Enchanted Forest, the seven-year effort of Roger Tofte, the man who designed and constructed this beautiful world of make-believe. And the Enchanted Forest is an easy detour for either the short or long version of this loop.

Begin at Bush Park, just south of downtown Salem. Cycle through the park to Davidson Street. Turn left on Wilbur, right on Berry, another right on Rural, and a left on Summer Street. This is the route of a Bike Way which will eventually have signs indicating the turns. At Hoyt Street turn left, crossing 13th Street, onto Pringle Road. Follow Pringle south, up and down its inclines, even after it changes into Battle Creek Road, and after it becomes an isolated windy

route cutting through groves of oak, willow, and pine.

After about 7¾ miles you will intersect Delany Road, also called the Turner-Sunnyside Road. Turn right for the detour to the Enchanted Forest. If some of the inclines are too steep for your bicycling legs, do not be afraid to walk them; the scenery is just as enjoyable on foot as it is on wheels.

To the east of the Enchanted Forest is Turner, a town settled more than one hundred years ago that has grown up around its main industry: a lumber mill. Visitors can view the entire mill operation, from the dumping of logs into the pond, to the transporting of them into the mill, to the burning of waste in the rusty wigwam burner.

For riders taking the short loop version, this town marks the turning point. Proceed north on Turner Road, past the white penitentiary on the knoll, past the dog pound. A little farther is Cascade Park, a large development with facilities for swimming, and picnicking.

From Cascade Park a bicycle path follows the west side of the road. Use this path for it provides a degree of protection when the traffic increases near the city, and it offers a convenient means of negotiating the Mission Street intersection. Make a right on 25th Street to Simpson Street, near the railroad tracks. Turn right again on 24th Street to Mills, where you turn left. Follow Mills to Winter and turn left to Bush Park. This section of streets is designated to become an official Bike Route and avoids much of the traffic on the main arteries.

Riders of the long loop version should bicycle through the town of Turner east on the Turner-Aumsville Road. At Aumsville, small Porter Boone Park has picnicking facilities in the wooded section at the rear. From Aumsville ride north on the Aumsville Highway which parallels the Santiam Highway for a distance. The 1971 National Bicycle Racing Championships took place along a part of this road near Western Baptist Bible College.

Cross over the Santiam Highway and at State Street turn left. Follow State into Salem, turning left at 23rd Street. Here, the very visible green signs of a Bike Route begin to direct you back to Bush Park.

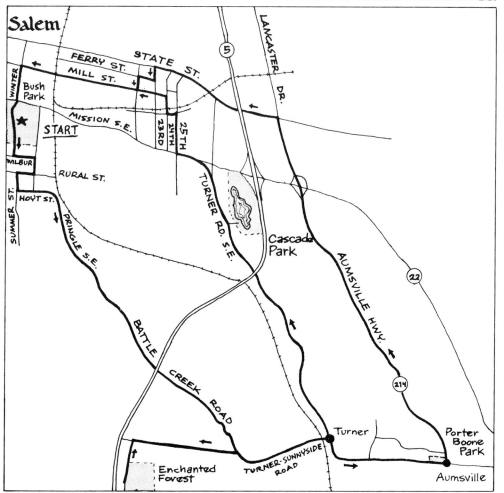

General location: near Monmouth, 14 miles south of Salem on Highway 99W
Distance:
  short loop: 16½ miles
  long loop: 33½ miles
Riding time:
  short loop: ±2 hours
  long loop: ±3½ hours
Traffic conditions: nonexistent to light
Road conditions: mostly level; short section of gravel
Ride rating:
  short loop: **
  long loop: ***

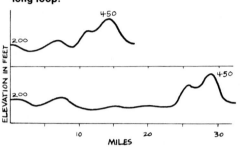

Buena Vista Ferry, Ankeny National Wildlife Refuge, the quiet town of Independence and its riverside park, and Monmouth with its 100-year-old college await you on this bicycle loop. The short version takes you to the ferry and Buena Vista Park; the long version through part of the wildlife refuge.

It all starts at the Oregon College of Education in Monmouth. Near the corner of Church Street and Monmouth Avenue is what remains of Campbell Hall, the oldest building on campus. The Columbus Day wind storm in October, 1962 toppled the building's tower and leveled a grove of fir trees nearby. but the 130-foot Sierra Redwood, which locals fondly refer to as the "World's Tallest Living Christmas Tree," still stands.

Bicycle south on Monmouth Avenue two blocks to Main Street and turn to the left. Follow Main until it becomes Oregon 51, headed for Independence. On both sides of this wide street there are clearly marked bike lanes which continue on into Independence.

In Independence, turn to the right at

Near Ankeny Wildlife Reserve

the end of Oregon 51, at the corner of the reconditioned city bank. Head south on this road. About 4½ miles from the starting point the road forks. Take the road on the left, the one in the direction of the sign saying "Wigrich." There is soon a rather steep escarpment, some 20 feet high, in the terrain. This drop indicates the level to which the Willamette used to flood. The land below the escarpment was frequently underwater before the days of flood control. Now it is productive farmland. All kinds of crops can be seen growing in this area, everything from filberts to corn.

Go through Wigrich, through Hopeville, on through Modeville, until you reach Buena Vista. Proceed toward the ferry, but if you want to take a break, stop off at the adjacent park. Picnic facilities are available. And so is a flock of tame fowl.

For the short loop, the journey has reached its midpoint. Follow the instructions given in the long version to return to Monmouth. For the long loop, cross the river on the ferry. Look for the blue herons that sometimes frequent these waters.

On the other side of the river bicycle toward Sidney, another town in name only. If there is a breeze in the air you are liable to be entertained by the telephone lines resonating at audible frequencies.

At Sidney turn to the right toward Talbot, a town with both a church and a general store. Bear right (west) at the Talbot intersection to return to the ferry. After Buena Vista go in the opposite direction from where you came earlier: proceed south and then west.

After a short distance the main road turns to the left, but you should continue straight, over a slight incline and through a paved but rough section of road. This roughness continues for about one-half mile and then changes into a well-surfaced, slightly used and somewhat hilly paved road heading north. Follow it all the way back to Independence, where you might want to stop off at the park on the north end of town, and on to Monmouth.

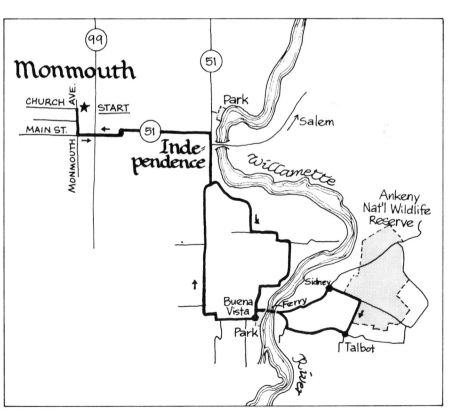

General location: 33 miles north of Salem off Interstate 5
Distance:
   short loop: 16½ miles
   long loop: 25½ miles
Riding time:
   short loop: ±2 hours
   long loop: ±3 hours
Traffic conditions: nonexistent to light
Road conditions: level
Ride rating:
   short loop: *
   long loop: ***

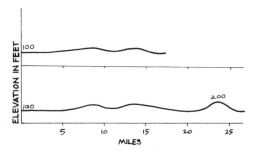

Gasoline pump near Champoeg

One site in Oregon is more steeped in historical tradition than any other. One site is more abundant in historical museums as well as park and recreation areas than any other. One site provides all of this and a beautiful bicycle loop in addition. The site is Champoeg State Park, located about 25 miles north of Salem, just west of Interstate 5, along the Willamette River.

It was at Champoeg that Oregon's first provisional government was formed in 1843 and the state constitution written. The vote was close, however, with 50 of the 102 settlers present voting against establishing a local government. Fur trappers and pioneers were not the type willing to impose governmental regulations on their affairs. It was also at Champoeg that the Hudson's Bay Company established one of its far-reaching tentacles — a trading post and grain storage. An Oregon governor in 1900 bicycled the distance from Salem to nearby Butteville especially to attend a meeting to determine if Champoeg should be designated a historical site.

Now Champoeg is a state park with three museums. One is a replica of a pioneer log cabin, built by the Daughters of the American Revolution in 1931. Despite what one thinks of the sponsoring organization, this cabin and the pioneer relics inside are of considerable interest. The Newell House, located just outside the park entrance, is also very worthwhile to visit. There are huge spinning wheels, oak dressers that were shipped around the Horn, New York newspapers proclaiming Lincoln's assassination, and a great old cast iron kitchen stove. It is all there, just as it was more than one hundred years ago.

After taking time to see the sites within the park, bicycle out the entrance and turn right. This loop, of which there is a short and a long version, takes you by rich farmland planted with grain seeds, fields of hops with their vines suspended from a high netting of wires, past some spectacular views of the Willamette, and down some plain, ordinary country roads excellent for bicycling.

Follow the road as indicated on the map. You will reach St. Paul after 11 miles, a good place for a rest. Oregon's first Catholic church was built here in 1836. A miniature replica of that original log building stands next to the present church.

Bicycle out of St. Paul toward the east, the same direction you were traveling before. About two miles up the road there is a route back to Champoeg, the route to bicycle to complete the short version of this loop. Follow the road back to the park entrance.

To bicycle the longer version, disregard the intersection and continue bicycling straight ahead for about 3½ miles, to where the road ends. Turn left and head north toward the town of Donald. This little town seems quiet on the surface, but when you get to talking to the general store proprietor you will find out the place is infested with political division. City council questions on whether to construct a sewer system and enact regulations regarding septic tanks cause tempers to boil. This town of 200 resorted to recalling its city council not many years back, so vehement were the political disagreements between Donald's citizens.

From Donald proceed north toward Butteville, a near ghost town settlement, except for the 81-year-old general store keeper and, according to this lady, her neighbor across the street "who is older than God himself."

To return to Champoeg, leave Butteville by the same road you came in, turning right at the intersection with the sign pointing in the direction of the park.

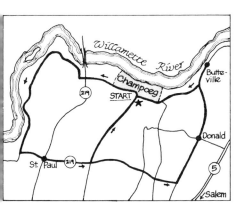

61

General location: Salem area
Distance:
   short loop: 32 miles
   long loop: 48 miles
Riding time:
   short loop: ± 3 hours
   long loop: ± 4½ hours
Traffic conditions: light to moderate
Road conditions: mostly level
Ride rating:
   short loop: ***
   long loop: ****

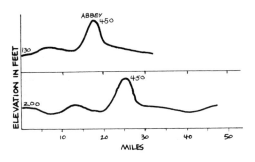

Church at Mt. Angel

Shop signs in German, store fronts resembling those common to Swiss villages, a Gothic church structure, an abbey featuring Benedictine Monks. No, you have not been transplanted to some village in Switzerland. You are still in Oregon, very near Salem. You are in the town of Mt. Angel, the destination of this bicycle loop. And, if you decide to take this tour during a four-day period in late September, you will be treated to an Old World beer drinking festival — Oktoberfest. Bicycle races, as well as many other forms of entertainment, are scheduled then.

As with many of the other loops in this book, there are two versions to this ride. One starts at Bush Pasture Park near downtown Salem; the shorter version begins at the intersection of Portland Road and Hazel Green Road, near the Chemawa Indian School, on the north side of Salem. For people taking the short version, you can reach the starting point by driving in your car the route suggested for bicyclists orginating at Bush Pasture Park, or you can consult a Salem street map for a faster, more direct route. Park your car near the starting point and follow the adjacent map and text below.

For the long version, leave Bush Park on Winter Street, heading north. Turn right on Mill Street, following the Bike Route signs posted along the way. At 17th Street, turn left and follow it to Silverton Road. The county fairgrounds are on the right-hand corner. Turn right, passing under Interstate 5, until coming to the next street, Fisher Road. Turn left on it until it ends at Ward, where you make a right, and then a left on Lancaster Drive. Remain on Lancaster until it merges with Portland Road, where a bicycle path begins.

Follow the bike path to Hazel Green Road. This intersection between Hazel Green and Portland Road is the starting point of the short version. Here, begin bicycling east on Hazel Green. Soon, all the traffic will be left behind, and you will be all to yourself, your friends, and nature.

Out in what may appear as open pasture is a flashing yellow street light. It marks the intersection with Howell-Prairie Road, where you turn left. Continue on Howell-Prairie for about 2½ miles until reaching Saratoga Road, where you turn to the right and follow the signs to Mt. Angel. In the distance you can sometimes see the Romanesque buildings of the abbey.

There is a railroad crossing just before the town center and, just after it, on College Street, the street heading toward the abbey, is St. Mary's Catholic Church, an imposing Gothic building.

St. Benedict's Abbey is about a mile outside of Mt. Angel, just beyond two tall residential buildings — a retirement home — and across from a field of hops. Turn right at the sign and climb the shaded lane. The Stations of the Cross are marked along the path. At the top of the knoll is the abbey.

Many of the abbey buildings are open to the public, and the very modern abbey library is especially worth visiting. But most of all, be sure to ask at the information desk for the key to the abbey museum, a small room in the basement of the main building. One of the small items awaiting you there is a massive stuffed moose head, hanging low enough from the wall for you to rub noses with the animal. The room is nearly overflowing with artifacts and museum miscellania — and some special surprises which we will let you discover.

From the abbey, turn to the right and follow the road around the eastern slope of the knoll. Turn right on Road 74 and right again at the next intersection. Follow this road, called Downs and later Route 634 and later still Labish Center Road, all the way to the Labish Center, site of a general store. Turn to the left and you will soon be back on Hazel Green Road. Follow it back to the intersection with Portland Road, starting point for the short version of the loop. For the long version, retrace the roads already described from here to Bush Pasture Park in Salem.

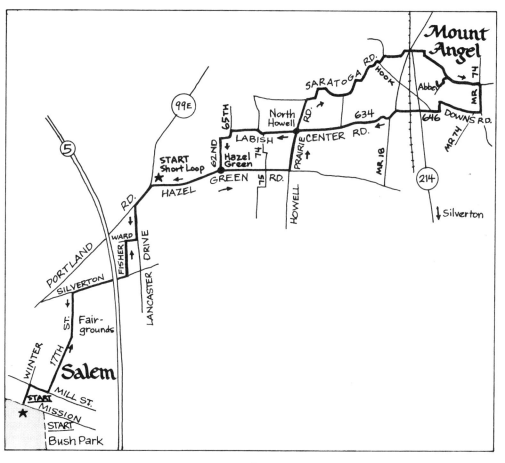

General location: Salem area
Distance:
   short loop: 38 miles
   long loop: 62½ miles
Riding time:
   short loop: 3½ hours
   long loop: 5 hours
Traffic conditions: light to moderate
Road conditions: long, straight sections with
   hills
Ride rating:
   short loop: ***
   long loop: ****

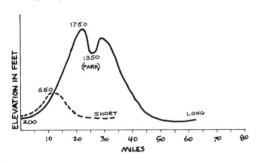

Silver Falls State Park

necessary for this ride, do not pass it up.

There is also a short version to the loop that does not get you to Silver Falls, but does pass by some pleasant farmland and stops in Silverton's City Park.

For both versions start at Bush Pasture Park in Salem, located just south of the downtown area, and begin bicycling north along Winter Street. Follow the Bike Route signs posted along the way. They will direct you through a series of turns: right on Mill Street, left on 21st, right on Ferry, left on 23rd, to State Street. The signs are easy to follow and mark the safest route to State Street.

Follow this road out of town, past the State Penitentiary and across Interstate 5, until it ends at an intersection with Cascade Highway. For the short version turn left on Cascade and bicycle in the direction of Silverton. A sign indicates it is 7 miles to the left. Follow the road into the town and head toward City Park, two blocks south of the crossing of Water and Main Streets, the main thoroughfares in Silverton, on Coolidge Street. This heavily-wooded park, situated along Silver Creek, is equipped with all the usual picnicking facilities. It is a fine place to stop.

For the long version, turn right on

The long version of this loop is strictly for the experienced cyclist. It is the longest route and has some of the steepest climbs charted on these pages. No doubt about it, it is a strenuous trip. But the consequent pleasures are proportional to the effort, for you visit Silver Falls State Park, one of the most scenic in Oregon. The canyon in which the park is situated has no less than 14 waterfalls, five with more than 100-foot drops. If you are in the physical shape

Cascade Highway and then immediately left on Victor Point Road. Proceed due east until reaching Victor Point, where you turn right and head south. In about 3½ miles you will intersect Highway 214. Turn left, heading east. This road is considerably busier than those ridden thus far, so bicycle cautiously. It also has a steep, long climb, but just beyond Ridge Road there is a nice descent.

Once in Silver Falls Park, stop at the information booth at the first campground entrance and pick up a folder that describes the park. It has a map locating hiking trails, waterfalls, and picnic facilities.

For the return trip, continue bicycling on Highway 214 in the direction of Silverton. There are a number of falls close to the road you may wish to stop and view. Exercise caution once out of the park, especially on the descent into Silverton. Once in Silverton go to City Park. There is an entrance to the park from the road on which you enter Silverton (now called

South Water Street), next to the public library.

To return to Salem leave the park and at Main Street cross over to McClaine Street which is just to the right. This is also called Highway 213 and the Silverton Road. Signs clearly indicate the direction to Salem. Follow this road to Howell-Prairie Road and turn left. There is a blinking red light above the intersection, an elementary school on one corner and a gas station on another.

Bike south on Howell-Prairie to Sunnyview Road (Route 720) and turn right. Follow this road into Salem. In the wide section near town, it is permissible to bicycle on the sidewalk which has curb cuts at the corners. Turn left on the intersection with Lancaster Street. At the next signal, leave Lancaster, turn right on "D" Street. Remain on "D" to 17th Street, where you turn left. Take 17th past State Street to Mill Street and follow the bike signs from here back to Bush Park.

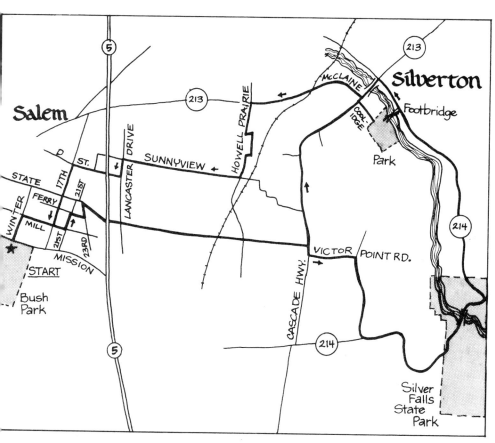

26 CORVALLIS-PHILOMATH LOOP

General location: Corvallis vicinity
Distance: 13 miles
Riding time: ±1½ hours
Traffic conditions: light
Road conditions: level
Ride rating: *

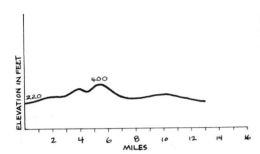

Philomath may seem like an insignificant town compared to nearby Corvallis. But it has some interesting history, some old buildings, and — once you get to talking — some friendly people. Philomath also provides a convenient stopping point on a nice, easy bicycle loop from Corvallis, a trip you could easily manage in two or three hours.

Start at Avery Park, located just south of the Oregon State University campus, across U.S. 20. If you have not already explored this park, take some time to do so now. It has deer, elk, and peacocks in a fenced area; spacious wooded picnic grounds; an old steam engine; rose gardens; and some very friendly old crows, always hinting for an invitation to join you for lunch.

Leave the park by the 15th Street exit, crossing Mary's River and the Corvallis-Newport Highway (U.S. 20). In another block you will come to Western Boulevard. Turn left and follow Western for about a mile. There is a sidewalk on the left side of the road which bicyclists may share with pedestrians. Just past 36th Street there is a fork in the road; bear to the right. The other route takes you to Oregon 34, the main — but busier — road to Philomath.

Follow this sometimes hilly West Hills Road to its end in Philomath. Along the way there are open fields, apple orchards, and various other crops. Chickens sometimes wander loose on the road, it is so seldom traveled.

Once in Philomath, turn left on Main Street. Soon you will see the most significant monument remaining in this century-old town — the old brick building of the now-defunct Philomath College. According to some senior citizens, who are nearly as old as the town, a group of United Brethren moved here from Indiana in 1853. Naming the town for two Greek words meaning "lover of learning," they almost immediately proceeded to build a college for their children. They made the bricks for the building on the spot and used huge timbers inside. In 1867 the college was opened and remained active until financial troubles shut it down in 1929. The building is now being renovated to make it into a museum and public library. Some of Philomath's citizens hope it may someday become a national monument.

Continue bicycling straight on Main Street until reaching 15th Street, across from the First National Bank. Turn right on 15th, bicycle for about seven blocks, and turn left at the crossing with Plymouth Road. There is a lumbering operation on the northwest corner. Remain on Plymouth Road past Bellfountain Road, until reaching S.W. 53rd, where you turn left. After about one-half mile there is a four-corner intersection with a power station on the far left corner. The street sign says "48-05." Turn right; in about another half mile you will pass a golf course. Turn left at the intersection with County Club Way, using the bike lane near the elementary school.

Soon you will come to a signal crossing with Oregon 34. Continue straight until the next intersection which is with S.W. Western Boulevard. With a right turn on Western, you are back on the home stretch. From here follow the route back to Avery Park.

Avery Park, Corvallis

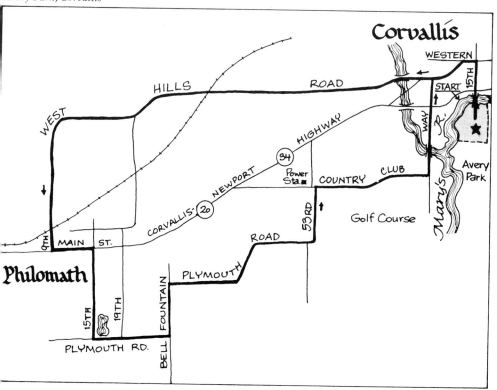

General location: Corvallis vicinity
Distance: 14 miles
Riding time: ± 1½ hours
Traffic conditions: light to moderate
Road conditions: plenty of bikeways
Ride rating: *

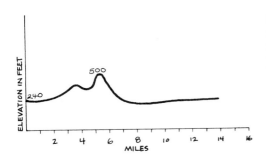

Corvallis is a town filled with well-preserved old buildings, tree-lined streets, and a pleasantness in the atmosphere that makes you glad you are there. This tour takes you by some of the historic buildings dotting the city and along some of the quiet streets where maple branches arch overhead. It also takes you out into the surrounding countryside, past walnut orchards, dairy pastures, and horse stables.

Start at the Memorial Union building on the Oregon State University campus. If you have not visited the campus before, take time to look around this very scenic university. Proceed east on Jefferson Avenue, the street in front of the Memorial Union. Turn left at the intersection just past the information booth located in the middle of the street. Off to the left is Benton Hall, the original building of the school. There is a tree-lined, paved walkway cutting across the lawn opposite Benton Hall. Turn on it, passing through the college gates onto Madison Avenue.

A few blocks down Madison, across from Central Park, is an old church built in the late 1800's, now serving as a community art center. Next to this art center is another well-preserved building of Victorian architecture. Turn left at 5th Street. To the right is the County Court House, erected in 1855, and still very much in use.

At Tyler Street make another left and follow to N. 11th Street. Both of these streets have been marked as bicycle lanes. In fact, as you bicycle around, it may seem as if all of Corvallis' streets have those special green signs along them. Certainly a good many of them do — all the routes connecting schools and parks in the city.

Follow 11th past Garfield School to Cleveland where you jog to the right to get on Highland Way. Continue bicycling north on Highland, past a blinking light warning motorists to be wary of pedestrians and bicyclists, up a slight hill and eventually over the crest down into the valley.

Highland Way ends at the intersection with Lewisburg Road. Turn right here until reaching Mountain View Drive in about 300 yards, where you turn left. Mountain View is a very scenic, somewhat hilly loop, ending up on U.S. 99W.

Bicycle south on U.S. 99, using its wide shoulder as a lane. In less than a mile, off to the left, is Elliot Road, a side route which parallels Highway 99, but is free of traffic. Follow it past the Lewisburg site, until it returns to U.S. 99.

Once again, travel on the main road until Ninth Street forks off to the right. Take it to N.E. Walnut, where you turn right and soon intersect Highland Way again. Follow the suggested route on the adjacent map to return to the OSU campus from here.

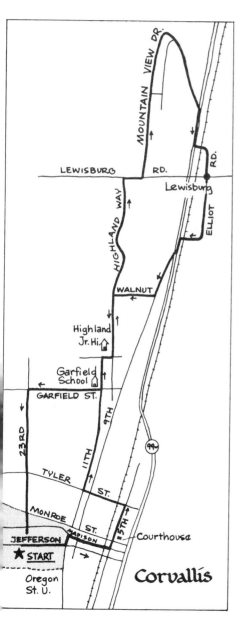

MOUNTAIN VIEW DR.

LEWISBURG   RD.   RD.

Lewisburg

HIGHLAND WAY

ELLIOT

WALNUT

Highland
Jr. Hi.

Garfield
School

GARFIELD ST.

9TH

23RD

11TH

99

TYLER   ST.

MONROE   ST.

15TH

MADISON

JEFFERSON   Courthouse

★ START

Oregon
St. U.

Corvallis

Oregon State University Campus

General location: Corvallis vicinity
Distance:
    short loop: 24 miles
    long loop: 41 miles
Riding time:
    short loop: ±2½ hours
    long loop: ±4 hours
Traffic conditions: light
Road conditions: flat
Ride rating:
    short loop: **
    long loop: ****

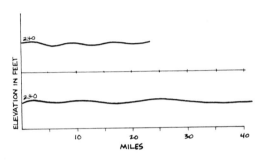

If you have never been up close to wheat and rye and other grains or if you have never experienced the flatness of farmland and the earthy smells that accompany it, this bicycle loop is a must for you. As with many of the other tours in this book, there is both a short and a long version; choose the one for which you are most in shape.

Both versions begin at the Corvallis bridges crossing the Willamette on Oregon 34. Cross the river, bicycling east on Oregon 34 about a mile until you reach the Peoria Road junction. Turn right and follow this road to the townsite of Peoria. Along the way you will pass fields planted with corn, beans, and a multitude of other vegetables, plus grains grown for seed. If you look closely, you will even spot swampy sections of Owl Creek, parts of it covered with water lillies, toads croaking somewhere underneath the vegetation.

Peoria was a stopping point for river traffic during the last century and is said to be one of the original settlements along the Willamette. The Peoria General Store, which sells everything from automobile fan belts to penny candy, is more than 90 years old. Sixty-foot hand-hewn beams support its spacious floor, and the store owner is more than willing to tell you the town's history and show you his private antique collection. He will also direct you back up the road to Peoria Park which "has a beautiful view of the river."

To return to Corvallis via the short loop, turn left at the street opposite the white sign announcing Peoria, an abandoned store on the opposite corner. Follow the road to the first intersection and turn left in the direction of Fayette and Shedd. At the next three-way intersection turn right and, shortly thereafter, left. Bicycle back this route, following the signs to Oakville and Corvallis.

For the long loop, take the same road as mentioned above out of Peoria, except head in the direction of Fayette and on to Shedd. Once arriving at the Shedd crossroads, you may be a bit disappointed not to find a booming metropolis. But there was a day when these streets bustled with activity, Shedd being a depot for wheat and cattle shipping. The Methodist Church in Shedd has been acknowledged as an historical monument of sorts. Services have been held there continuously since the building was completed in 1873. A block down the road is another church, but this one has been released from the hands of God into those of an antique dealer. It's a beautiful sun-bleached building, and the antiques inside are genuine; nothing plastic or twentieth-century here.

To return to Corvallis, go north on U.S. 99E for about two miles until reaching a road to the left with a sign saying Oakville and Verdune. Follow that road and the signs to Oakville, and note yet another church — this one built in 1850 — on a knoll overlooking the Oakville intersection. Take the road leading north here, and at its end, about a mile up the way, turn left and proceed back to Corvallis.

Oakville

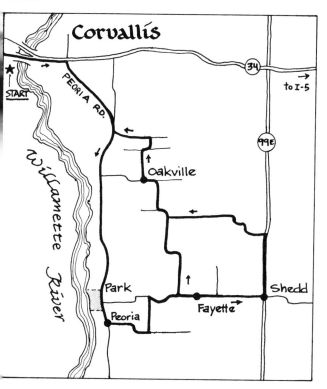

29 CORVALLIS-ALBANY LOOP

General location: Corvallis vicinity
Distance: 22 miles
Riding time: ±2 hours
Traffic conditions: light
Road conditions: flat
Ride rating: **

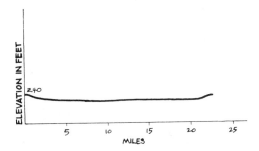

Around the turn of the century, Corvallis cyclists held races on their penny-farthings between Corvallis and Albany. They would get a willing farmer to smooth the ten-mile stretch of dirt with his horse-drawn plow and race away, the winner being awarded a dollar in prize money to be spent at his favorite general store.

Times have changed a bit: the road is paved now, the penny-farthings (those 1890 vintage bicycles with a very large diameter front wheel and small rear wheel) have been relegated to the museums. And the prize money — in large part because of inflation — has increased many fold whenever a race is held. Still, the Corvallis-Albany route is bicycled and enjoyed, but today more by Sunday leisure cyclists than by avid racers.

The most scenic and lightly traveled route is along Riverside Drive. Start the tour at Oregon State University. Head east on Jefferson to 5th Street, turning left until reaching Van Buren. Cross one of the bridges spanning the Willamette on Oregon 34 heading east. Bicycle on the wide shoulder of this sometimes busy road.

After a mile from the bridge you will pass the Barn Theatre on the right; in another mile and a half, Colorado Lake Drive will veer off to the left. Nearly three miles from the bridges, there is a large green highway sign announcing Riverside Drive to the left.

Turn onto this road, leaving the traffic behind on Oregon 34. Follow this windy, flat road past an old cemetery and abandoned church, and yet another cemetery a little further along. Giant oaks line much of this quiet road and the ranch house farmers living along it seem to enjoy planting large vegetable gardens and selling their produce from frontyard stands.

About 8 miles from the Corvallis bridges, Riverside Drive intersects Bryant Drive: turn left here. This little diversion will take you past fields of pole beans and, within 2½ miles, Bryant Park, located just inside the Albany city limits. This park offers a fine place to stop and picnic: woods, picnic tables, grass, and a view of the Willamette.

Follow the same route in reverse to return to Corvallis.

Oregon State University

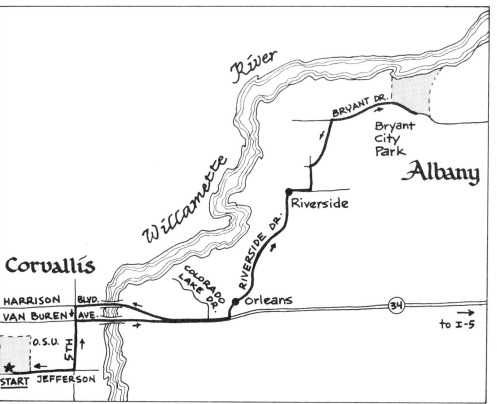

River

Willamette

BRYANT DR.

Bryant
City
Park

Albany

Riverside

RIVERSIDE DR.

Corvallis

COLORADO
LAKE DR.

Orleans

HARRISON BLVD.

VAN BUREN AVE.

34

to I-5

O.S.U.

5TH

START JEFFERSON

General location: Albany vicinity
Distance:
  short loop: 19 miles
  long loop: 24 miles
Riding time:
  short loop: ±2 hours
  long loop: ±2½ hours
Traffic conditions: light
Road conditions:
  short loop: flat
  long loop: few hills
Ride rating:
  short loop: **
  long loop: **

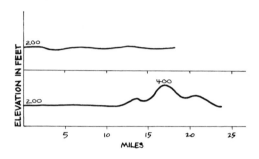

Waverly Park is one of Albany's two major parks. This one comes equipped with a pond, where some domesticated mallards make their home. Located just west of I-5 and the Albany Municipal Airport, it serves as a convenient starting place for this bicycle loop winding through Albany farmland.

Proceed north along the Old Salem Highway. After about 2 miles, turn left in the direction of Millersburg and Willamette Memorial Park. In another mile is a four-way intersection, with Southern Pacific oil tanks on the far right corner and the Millersburg Market on the left. Turn here, on N.E. Conser Road.

Continue on Conser Road, taking in the many farms and pastures and orchards. Occasionally you will see the dwellings provided the men and women who pick the produce from these fields. Remember these migrant labor camps next time you hear of farm workers striking for higher wages and better working conditions.

N.E. Conser eventually becomes N.E.

Dever Connor Road. At the first possible chance, turn off of it to the left onto N.E. Cooper Road, a paved but very narrow road, hardly wide enough for a modern tractor to negotiate. This road will take you past some really pleasant backwoods farmhouses.

At the next intersection beyond the railroad tracks, turn left onto N.E. Harnish Road. More farmland up ahead. In awhile you will come to a three-way intersection with a sign indicating N.E. Hoefer Road to the right. Take it. In a few tenths more you will come to yet another intersection and the site of the old Conners School, now an abandoned, run-down, boarded-up little white building. This school and intersection mark the separation of the short and long versions of this loop.

For the short loop, follow along Hoefer Road, making all the necessary jogs in the road due to property lines. Soon you will pass an exquisite farmhouse, with a barn across from it. It is owned by an elderly couple who dutifully plant a large garden each season and sell produce from their own little frontyard market. Such a pleasure to do business and talk with these people! This loop continues along, eventually reaching the oil tanks passed miles ago. Follow the same road back to Waverly Park as you bicycled out.

The long loop separates off at Conners School site, passes over Interstate 5, and bends around and up a short hill overlooking the Santiam River. At the top of the knoll is a small art gallery, called "The Chalet." The owner, a man who used to farm most of the land around here, is something of a collector of Indian and early settler lore, as well as a craftsman in leather. He can show you where wagons would pull up for the ferry at the bend in the river, the wagon wheel ruts still visible to the trained eye. And under the large oak near the art gallery — that's where early settlers would often camp before continuing northward.

Bicycle down the hill, cross Jefferson Road Highway, the railroad tracks, and climb Hardscrabble Hill. Continue straight to Knox Butte School on the left and the intersection with Knox Butte Road. Turn right and head back toward Waverly Park.

Willamette River

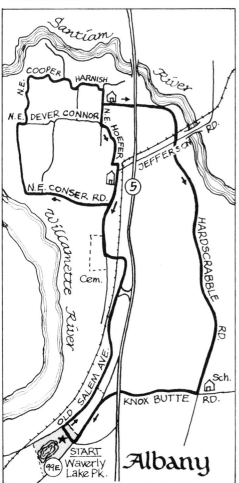

General location: Albany
Distance:
  short loop: 12 miles
  long loop: 18½ miles
Riding time:
  short loop: ± 1 hour
  long loop: ± 1½ hours
Traffic conditions: light
Road conditions: flat with some hills
Ride rating:
  short loop: *
  long loop: **

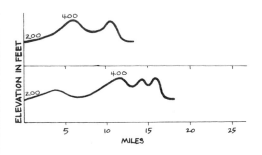

Contrary to what some people may think, Albany is more than a smelly pulp plant on Interstate 5. Albany has fine parks, old majestic houses and churches, quiet residential areas, and a surrounding region and road system well suited to bicycling.

One of the nicest loops in this area starts at the foot of Albany's two bridges crossing the Willamette River. These bridges are located in the heart of Albany and are part of U.S. 20. Cross the northbound bridge (there is a wide shoulder and an elevated pedestrian walk) and bicycle to the intersection of U.S. 20 and Spring Hill Road. Turn right on Spring Hill, traveling by the golf course to the right. Just after the golf course is a paved section (separated from the road by a mound of asphalt) which pedestrians and bicyclists may use.

After two more miles there is yet another golf course along the road, on the left-hand side. But soon these structured forms of recreation are left behind, replaced by open pasture, fields of ryegrass, corn, and other crops. Sometimes, through the brush, you can see the Willamette River slowly making its meandering way north to the Columbia.

Five and a half miles from Albany is an intersection with Fir Grove Road. Fir Grove Elementary School is located on the corner. Turn left here if you intend to bicycle the short loop. Continue on Fir Grove Road to Palestine Church Road, at which point the long loop joins this road.

For the long loop, bear right at the Fir Grove Road intersection. A quarter of a mile down the road is a barn being run over by blackberry bushes and a beautiful, unpainted farm house, both still very much in use.

At two intersections you may be enticed to turn toward Buena Vista and Independence. Resist at both spots and remain on the same road, even as it bends to the left, taking you in a southerly direction. In about two miles is an intersection. Take the road plainly marked, headed in the direction of Palestine.

Palestine Church Road, a little hilly, passes what is described by the billboard as "Christmas Tree Plantation," and it surely must be, given the number and variety of living-room-size conifers growing here. Continue straight and up a slight incline, past an intersection with Palestine Road, until reaching North Palestine Memorial Church. This white, clapboard building stands alone on a wooded knoll overlooking the farmland through which you have just bicycled. The simplicity of the building, the peacefulness of the area, and the beauty of the view make this a delightful stopping spot. The grounds are open and covered with grass. There are even two outhouses with real wooden seats, unlike the plastic variety found in state parks.

Continue straight on Palestine Church Road to Fir Grove Road and turn to the right. It is here the short version intersects the long loop. Follow this road straight, over another small hill, and eventually onto what is called "Scenic Drive." You will climb a short hill and pass yet another golf course.

After coming down the other side of the hill, turn left on Thorton Lake Drive, just before the railroad tracks and U.S. 20. Thorton Lake Drive ends at Albany Road, where you turn right, cross the tracks and head once again toward Highway 20. But again, there is a side street just before Highway 20 which is much more enjoyable to ride. And on the corner, surrounded by trees and bushes, is the old home of an early settler in the area, William Peacock.

This street ends after a few blocks, merging with the first road you bicycled on, just across from the first golf course you passed. Turn right and cross the bridge to return to the starting point.

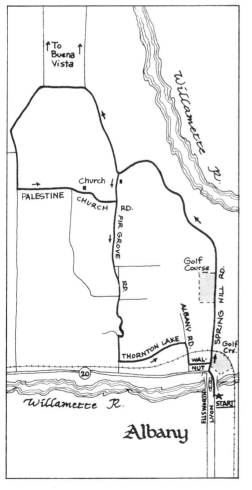

Willamette River

32 LEBANON-WATERLOO PARK LOOP

General location: Lebanon
Distance:
  short loop: 14½ miles
  long loop: 32½ miles
Riding time:
  short loop: ±1½ hours
  long loop: ±3 hours
Traffic conditions: light
Road conditions: level with some hills
Ride rating:
  short loop: *
  long loop: ***

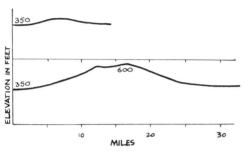

Both midway and at the end of this loop-within-a-loop, splendid parks await the bicycle traveler. The park in Waterloo, shaded by tall Douglas fir, is situated along the Santiam River and offers skinny dipping in the river and picnicking at the tables. At the far tip of the long loop is McDowell Park, replete with waterfalls, nature trails, old fashioned water pumps, picnic tables and fire pits. Both parks are very beautiful and very much worth bicycling to.

Begin both versions of this loop in Lebanon at Main Street and W. Academy, at the corner with Lebanon Jr. High and St. Edward's Church. Bicycle south on Main to Milton Street; turn left to Franklin Street and follow this narrow, quiet lane for the five-mile ride to Waterloo Park.

Waterloo was christened after its historical counterpart after an important court decision favoring one of the litigants. It is now a small settlement of

McDowell Park

peaceful folks seldom resorting to the courts to settle disputes. Bicyclists taking the short loop must pass through the town, crossing the bridge and cycling about a mile further to the intersection with the road heading back to Lebanon.

For people taking the long loop, proceed past the bridge, heading away from the river. Almost two miles from the park is an unmarked road, just before the railroad tracks and Highway 20. Turn left on this road, which eventually becomes McDowell Creek Road. In a short distance you will pass the site of the old Waterloo railroad station, its sign still standing.

Continue bicycling this road, following the signs to McDowell Park. Turn left at the corner marked with a white Mennonite Church on one side of the street and an elementary school opposite it. Cross the South Santiam River on a new concrete span which replaced a covered bridge.

In another mile is McDowell School. The park is straight ahead, up a few hills, but none that is really difficult. You'll agree, once there, that the 16 miles of bicycling was worth it — gurgling stream, a multitude of falls, ferns and cedar trees aplenty, and just lovely, lovely scenes.

To return to Lebanon, follow the road on the east bank of the Santiam. Cross the bridge entering Lebanon on Grant Street. Turn right on Park Street for the remaining few blocks left before returning to the starting point of this loop.

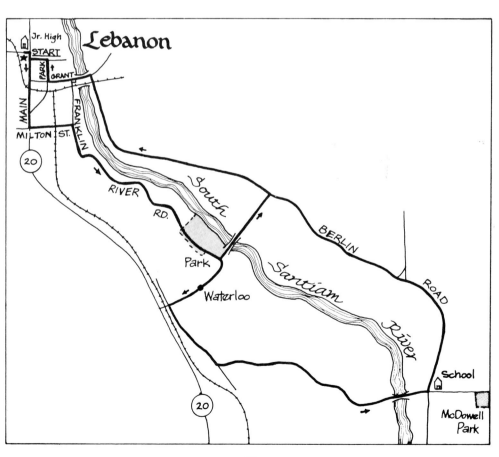

33 LEBANON-CRABTREE LOOP

General location: Lebanon vicinity
Distance: 21 miles
Riding time: ±2 hours
Traffic conditions: light
Road conditions: completely flat
Ride rating: **

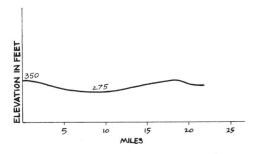

There was a time — about 60 years ago — when apple trees covered the acreage northeast of Lebanon. More than 2,000 acres were planted with apple seedlings, one of the greatest speculative schemes to hit Linn County. And now, not a productive tree. Plenty of scrawny, deformed ones though. This bicycle loop takes you through some of that territory and through the town of Crabtree, which derives its name not from the one-time apple venture, but from an early settler with that handle.

This tour also passes through some lovely farming country and by enough abandoned barns and homesteads to build a sizeable ghost town, were they all in one place. But not all the barns and buildings are abandoned; some, despite sagging roofs, missing shingles, and broken windows are still in everyday use. It's all to be seen on this loop to Crabtree.

Start at the Lebanon Junior High School park, located at the corner of Main Street (U.S. 20) and W. Academy (Oregon 34). It's the intersection of the two main highways passing through Lebanon. There is a community swimming pool on one end of the block and St. Edward's Catholic Church at the other end, across the street.

From there, proceed north on U.S. 20 one block to Wheeler Street and turn right. Follow this street past the sewage treatment center, past orchards and farms, until reaching a T-crossing. A sign indicates Tennessee School to the right; follow that route. There is another T-crossing in another mile; bear right again. Tennessee School appears 4½ miles from town, across a short bridge. There is a road heading north just before the bridge; take that road. Follow it and the signs directing you toward Crabtree.

Crabtree is about 11 miles from Lebanon and consists of little more than a church, a general store, and a tavern. But just outside Crabtree on the right-hand side of the road are hundreds of one-room dwellings for roosters. Quite a sight for someone unaccustomed to the peculiarities of chicken raising.

About a mile out of Crabtree is the turnoff back to Lebanon, plainly marked with a giant green highway sign: "Lebanon 8 miles." Follow this road through Griggs, past a large log pond where you can sometimes see workers balancing on the logs with their long poles in hand. Pass Brewster and its general store, and bicycle down into Lebanon. Cross the bridge into the city, following Grant Street through town to the Highway 20 and 34 turnoff. After nine more blocks of bicycling north on Park Street you will find yourself back at St. Edward's Church, the site from which you started this tour.

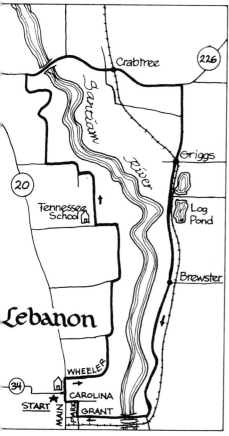

34 EUGENE-SPRINGFIELD BIKE TRAIL

General location: along Willamette River, between Eugene and Springfield
Distance: 7 miles round trip
Riding time: ¾ hour
Traffic conditions: no auto traffic on bike path
Road conditions: level
Ride rating: *

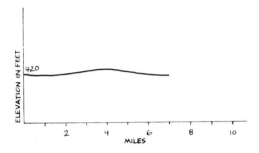

Only superlatives can adequately describe the specially designed Eugene-Springfield bike trail. It is a model for such trails. Constructed from the one percent state funds set aside for bicycle and hiking trails in Oregon, it features many rest stops along the Willamette River from Eugene's Alton Baker Park to Island Park in Springfield.

From park-to-park, the trail is less than four miles — a distance even great grandmothers should be able to bicycle with ease. But this trail should not be disregarded by seasoned riders because of its shortness. No trail is comparable, scenically, nor so close and convenient to Eugene and Springfield.

The trail starts at Alton Baker Park in Eugene over the Willamette River on the north side of the Ferry Street Bridge. This park is just off Centennial Boulevard, the road which goes to Autzen Stadium.

From the park head east along the river on the paved path. Soon you will leave the park and enter a wooded section restricted to bicyclists and pedestrians. Numerous waysides dot the path, convenient places to stop and relax, picnic or fish. At some points hiking paths lead into the woods.

The city's master plan indicates that eventually a park area will border much of the trail. One of these areas under development used to be the city dump. It is slowly being converted into rolling hills of green, the hills composed of refuge collected over many, many years.

Not far along, there is a concrete footbridge crossing the Willamette. This bridge, and the railroad underpass especially constructed for bicyclists and pedestrians, leads to the University of Oregon campus.

The main trail eventually merges with Garden Way, a secondary road which also follows the Willamette. Continue bicycling on Garden Way to Mill Street in Springfield (the first major street along this trail). Turn right. Two blocks later turn right again on 'B' Street. This street leads you into Springfield's Island Park, an expansive but yet secluded area with picnic tables, fire pits, and lots of shade. Return to Alton Baker Park in Eugene by retracing the above route.

Eugene Bike Trail

Alton Baker Park

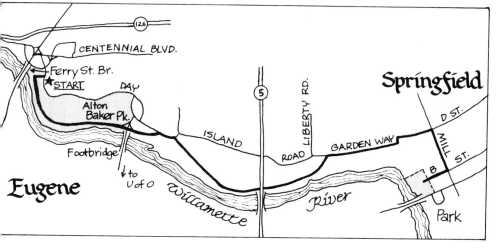

35 McKENZIE DRIVE LOOP

General location: Eugene area
Distance: 22½ miles
Riding time: ±2 hours
Traffic conditions: light
Road conditions: some hills
Ride rating: **

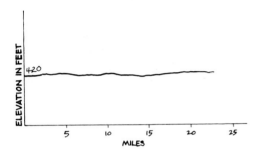

The Eugene area is favored with a number of backroads, relatively close to the city but far from its congestion. A network of them form this bicycle loop, a tour that takes you by three expansive parks, along both the McKenzie and Willamette Rivers, and along the very scenic Eugene-Springfield Bike Path.

Begin the loop at Alton Baker Park, located along the Willamette, just north of the Eugene downtown section, across the Ferry Street Bridge. This park is growing all the time and may some day house a velodrome — a specially built bicycle racing track.

Leave the park and bicycle north on Coburg Road to Harlow Road, where you turn right. Continue on Harlow, past Interstate 5, to Gateway Road, making a left at the intersection. Follow Gateway north, along some railway tracks, over the freeway again until reaching Armitage Road. Turn right on this road. The traffic is so infrequent along here that blackberry bushes have started to claim the shoulders of the road. This path (which dead-ends) takes you to the back section of Armitage Park. There is a gate you can pass through and plenty of places where the park fence has been matted down to permit crossing into the park.

From Armitage Park, cross the McKenzie River and turn right onto McKenzie View Drive. This is a somewhat hilly but very pleasant ride, with several scenic views of the river and adjacent farmland.

McKenzie View Drive terminates at an intersection with Hill Road. Turn right, cross the Mohawk River, and then turn right again onto Mohawk Road. Follow this quiet, country road to an intersection just before the McKenzie River. Cross over the river, following Marcola Road until it becomes 'Q' Street and parallels Interstate 105. Leave 'Q' at 5th Street, turning right at 'B' Street to reach Island Park, situated along the Willamette River.

The remainder of the loop is along the Eugene-Springfield Bike Path. Leave Island Park on 'B' Street, turning left on Mill to 'D' Street, where you turn left again. The path veers off this street (which eventually is called Garden Way). You'll enjoy the trip more if you stop occasionally along this wooded path and watch leaves float downstream or simply relax at the many way stations along the path. Alton Baker Park, the starting point, is directly ahead.

Along McKenzie Drive

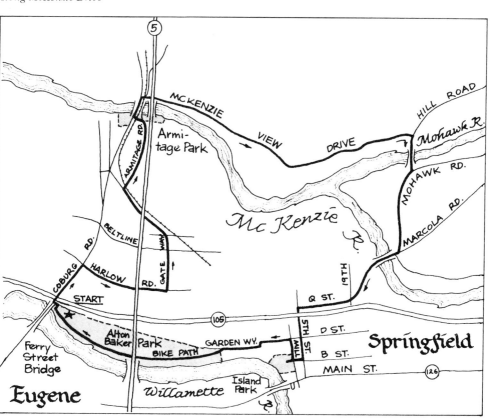

General location: Eugene
Distance: 9 miles
Riding time: ± 1 hour
Traffic conditions: light
Road conditions: steep climbs in Hendricks Park; bikeway along river
Ride rating: *

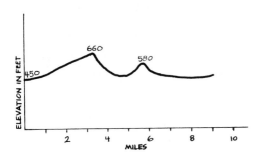

Hendricks Park must come close to resembling Paradise, its lush Rhododendron Gardens covering much of the hilltop park, its section of undisturbed wilderness except for a few hiking trails, its various deer species housed for viewing and feeding, its spacious picnic facilities.

But Hendricks Park, for all its beauty, is only one aspect of this bicycle loop. The University of Oregon campus — almost an arboretum in itself — is another significant attraction. And so is the Eugene-Springfield Bike Path.

Begin this loop at the University campus at the corner of University Avenue and 13th Street, the corner of the ERB Memorial Union. If you are not acquainted with the campus, take time to become so now. The section of 13th Street running through campus is closed to auto traffic; feel free to bicycle anywhere in this section and along the paved paths linking campus buildings. Deady Hall, the original structure of the University, nearly 100 years old, is still standing and in daily use. Several other interesting buildings, an art museum, and plant specimens cover this peaceful campus.

Leave the campus by way of University Avenue, traveling south to 21st Street. Turn left on 21st Street and ride right through a small park onto Fairmount Boulevard. Follow it to Summit Street and look for signs indicating Hendricks Park. The upcoming hill is fairly steep; no shame in walking to the top, the site of the park. In the main park area you will find a nice, invigorating road to the very top of the knoll. It loops past the animal cages and back to the picnic area. Try it.

Leave the park by Floral Hill Road, on the western side of the park. Soon a small valley comes into view. Follow Floral Hill around until it becomes Riverview Street. At 26th Street, turn right and then left on Augusta to Laurel Hill Drive, where you make a right. Climb this steep hill which parallels Interstate 5. (Again, you can cover the same ground by walking; it'll take just a little longer.) There is a moderately old cemetery at the top of this hill, after you cross the freeway.

Go down the other side, across the tracks, past the steel industry, into what is known as Glenwood. This little neighborhood has a distinctive Oklahoman flavor, many of the residents having moved from there long ago. An elderly bearded plumber lives in the area. Consistently dressed in striped overalls, he often goes to his jobs around the area on his ancient three-speed Raleigh, plumbing tools and parts jangling in his basket.

Turn east on 19th Street to Franklin Boulevard, where you turn left and then right across the Willamette River. Once across the river, turn right into Island Park.

From the park, bicycle toward the Eugene-Springfield Bike Path by leaving on 'B' Street, turning left on Mill, left again on 'D' until reaching the path. Return to the University of Oregon from the path by way of the footbridge spanning the Willamette just north of the University. Note the special railroad underpass especially built to accommodate bicyclists and pedestrians.

University of Oregon Campus

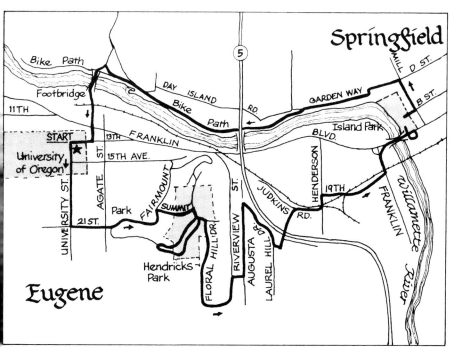

37 MOHAWK LOOP

General location: northeast of Eugene-Springfield
Distance:
  short loop: 13 miles
  long loop: 24 miles
Riding time:
  short loop: ± 1½ hours
  long loop: ± 2½ hours
Traffic conditions: light
Road conditions: mostly level
Ride rating:
  short loop: *
  long loop: **

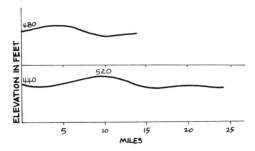

There is something very pleasant about bicycling along and waving to farmers cultivating their land, or watching sheep nibble grass, and viewing the quiet, very natural activity taking place in the valley below. It gives one a sense of reassurance in these troubled times that good is possible and exists, sometimes tucked away in small valleys such as this one.

There are two versions to this bicycle loop. The long version begins at Island Park in Springfield, located along the Willamette River, next to the bridge going into Springfield from Eugene. The short version begins at a bridge across the McKenzie River on Marcola Road. A small parking area where fishermen leave their riverboat trailers has room for bicyclists unhitching their two-wheelers from their auto carrier racks. This starting point, situated next to Town and Country School, is best reached by following the map for the long loop.

For the long version, leave Island Park via "B" Street to N. 5th, turning left on 5th. Pass through town, under Interstate 105, to Hayden Bridge Road, turning right. Lovely filbert orchards line the route along here. Hayden Bridge Road is

Near Mohawk

disconnected; you'll have to do some jogging along N. 19th and N. 20th to reach the second part. Along this section are more orchards and a shaded fruit stand, a small, family-owned enterprise.

After a small hill, this road intersects Marcola Road. Turn left and cross the McKenzie River. On the other side, there are three roads to choose from; take the one on the far left. It is almost absent of traffic and passes along some very pleasant farmland. Called Mohawk Road, it intersects Hill Road after about 1½ miles. Turn left on Hill, cross a small creek, and follow it all the way into Mohawk, a town site that has a store, a church, and an elementary school.

Cross Marcola Road onto what is called Sunderman Road. This pleasant, narrow route winds along the Mohawk River — more creek than a respectable river — and past the Springfield Country Club.

At the end of Sunderman, follow Marcola Road for about one mile until it intersects Old Mohawk Road. Here a sign points in the direction of Mohawk and the McKenzie Grange. Bicycle along this route, past Hill Road, where you turned off earlier, back to the McKenzie River and the starting point for the short loop. To return to Island Park in Springfield, simply follow the earlier route along Hayden Bridge Road.

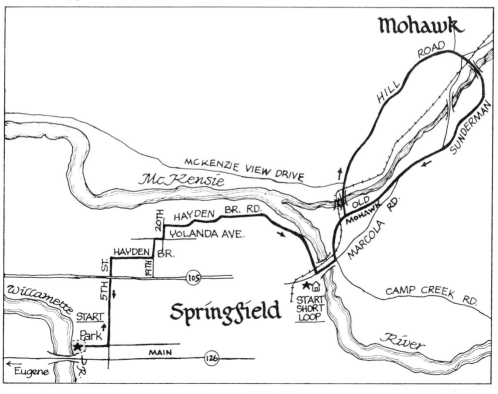

General location: Springfield and southeast
Distance:
   short route: 21 miles
   long route: 36 miles
Riding time:
   short route: 2 hours
   long route: 3½ hours
Traffic conditions: light to moderate
Road conditions: level
Riding rating:
   short route: **
   long route: ****

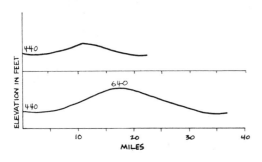

The Eugene-Springfield area has many possibilities for bicycle riding. One of the nicest rides, originating from and leading out of Springfield, is along the old Jasper-Lowell Highway. It is a flat, seldom traveled road which winds along the Willamette River, providing some very pleasant scenery.

The easiest starting point is Island Park in Springfield, located just over the bridge into Springfield from Eugene. From the park, turn left on Mill Street, cycle for a couple of blocks until you reach 'E' Street, and then turn right. Follow this very plain residential street until it dead ends at 28th Street. Although not especially scenic, this part of the route avoids the sometimes heavy traffic on the main thoroughfare in Springfield.

At 28th, turn right, cycling the few blocks to Main Street. Here you will have to turn left and bicycle along this major artery until 32nd Street. There is a wide shoulder, providing safe bicycling.

Turn right at 32nd. This street soon becomes Jasper Road, bending left and passing by a quiet rural residential area one would not expect to find in Springfield's city limits. Here you will see signs stuck in front lawns advertising fresh eggs, rabbits, fryers, and horses for sale. Country living in a small way.

There are no intersections along the road, only a few curves, and no hills. About 8 miles out, you will reach Jasper, a town that has been around for nearly 100 years. There is a grange and a large general store in the town center.

Across the bridge in Jasper is Jasper Park, a good rest and turn around place for cyclists doing the short route. Immediately after crossing the bridge turn left on Jasper Park Road, into the park.

For persons bicycling the long route, continue along Jasper Road, which now is heading for the town of Fall Creek. About 11 miles out is an intersection. Pengra Road is straight ahead and goes over a wide, relatively new, concrete bridge. Follow Jasper Road left. In another half mile you will pass a beautiful covered bridge. Keep going straight; you will have the opportunity to bicycle through that bridge on the return trip.

Pass through Fall Creek; just outside the town is an intersection where you turn right. And in another mile on the right side of the road is Unity Park, a peaceful place to swim, fish, and relax.

For the return route, turn right outside the park, away from the direction you already bicycled. You will soon pass through a covered bridge with a major junction immediately beyond it. Turn right again (a sign says Pengra Road). An old section of the road angles to the right before the main road, and will take you through the covered bridge we spoke of earlier. (Both routes, however, will get you back to Jasper Road.) After the covered bridge, turn left onto the road you bicycled earlier, the Jasper-Lowell Road. Follow it back to Springfield, retracing the route.

Jasper Road

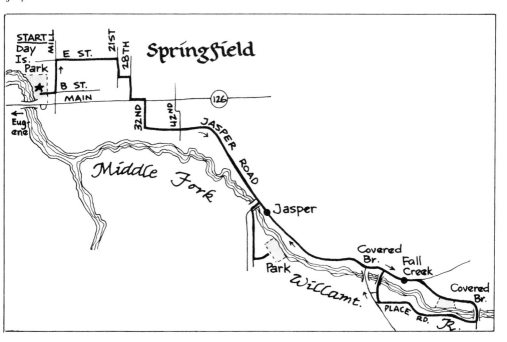

39 DORENA RESERVOIR LOOP

General location: east of Cottage Grove
Distance:
    short loop: 25 miles
    long loop: 43 miles
Riding time:
    short loop: ±2½ hours
    long loop: ±4 hours
Traffic conditions: light to moderate
Road conditions: two modest climbs; rest level
Ride rating:
    short loop: **
    long loop: ****

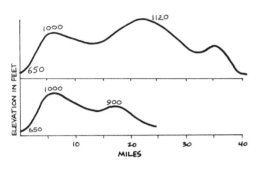

Some bicycle rides require special equipment: alpine gears, saddlebags for camping, etc. This loop does not require anything special, but a bathing suit or fish pole will make it all the more enjoyable. The swimming holes dotting Row River

at the end of Dorena Reservoir on the way to Disston are simply too enticing to pass up on a beautiful summer day.

Start this loop at the Village Green, a large motel and convention complex adjacent to Interstate 5, at the northeast edge of Cottage Grove. (Cottage Grove and the Village Green are located about 15 miles south of Eugene on Interstate 5; signs plainly indicate where to exit from the freeway.) The Village Green is also the station for "The Goose," the steam excursion train which daily during the summer chugs its way into the Bohemia mining region — another kind of trip well worth taking.

Head east on Row River Road from the Village Green. After about 3 miles of level riding you will pass a covered bridge on the right, one of two you will see on this trip. A fork in the road occurs about 4 miles from the start. Continue on Row River Road, taking the left branch of the fork.

Here you will encounter the most difficult incline of the loop. It is about a mile long and you will develop a healthy sweat climbing it. But at the top you can stop, relax, and look over the entire reservoir, enjoying quite a view.

Follow the road around the reservoir. Sometimes you may hear the shrill Goose train whistle and see a cloud of steam pouring from its engine. With only a slight leap of the imagination, this could become a scene from the late 1800's.

At the end of the reservoir, along Row River Road, is a second covered bridge, 12 miles from the point of departure. Here you have a choice: to relax, swim or fish in the river before riding through the bridge and back the other side of the reservoir, or to continue pedaling up the same road toward the small towns of Dorena and Disston. The road is paved, light in traffic, and easy to cycle. It is all up to you and your legs. (One enticement might be the Lasell S. Steward Recreation Site another 5½ miles up the road. This section of the river area has a giant pool, fed by a small waterfall — a lovely swimming and picnicking area.)

Whichever you choose, the return route is along Government Road on the south side of the reservoir. Follow it back to the intersection with Row River Road, turning left, which takes you back to the Village Green.

Dorena Reservoir

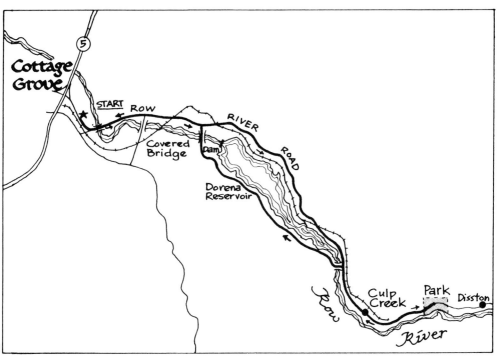

General location: Eugene and north to Junction City
Distance: 28½ miles
Riding time: ± 3 hours
Traffic conditions: moderate; sometimes heavy on River Road
Road conditions: level; bikeway on River Road
Ride rating: *

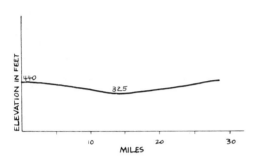

You don't have to be Scandinavian to enjoy the annual Scandinavian Festival held in Junction City each summer. It is one of the few festivals which has successfully avoided commercialization, and everything — except for food and craft items — is free: the exhibits, the dancing performances, the music, the tours of the surrounding region. It is a mighty exciting time to visit Junction City, a time when nearly all the citizenry dresses up in authentic Swedish, Norwegian, and Danish costumes. We highly recommend taking in the festival and combining your visit with a pleasant bicycle ride from Eugene.

Start this bicycle tour from Skinners Butte Park in Eugene, located along the Willamette River near the Ferry Street Bridge. The park is difficult to miss; it is part of the only large hill around which has a tall (and controversial) memorial cross on top of it. Skinners Butte Park itself is a pleasant place to bicycle, for it has bike and pedestrian paths that follow much of the river and extend to the city's rose gardens. The park is also the site of an annual bicycle race, usually held in late September.

Leave the park by way of Cheshire Street, turn left on Lawrence and then right on 1st Avenue. Follow 1st, which is sometimes busy, to River Road. There is a bike lane along much of this road, adding a welcome element of safety.

The farther you bicycle the less auto traffic there is, until near the city limits it diminishes to just an occasional car. About 5½ miles from the starting point is Awbrey Recreation Area, a nice wooded site on the right-hand side of the road. You will find picnic tables, firepits, and plenty of shaded lawn at this small park.

Continue straight on River Road toward Junction City. After about 14 miles of bicycling a pleasantly flat road surrounded by farmland and orchards, you will reach Junction City. Relax, look around this 100-year-old town (named after the early junction of two railroad lines), and take in the Scandinavian Festival if you are there at that time of year.

Leave Junction City along Highway 99, south in the direction of Eugene. In a little more than a mile, Prairie Road intersects this rather busy highway. Turn to the left on Prairie Road and enjoy yourself again, for motorists hardly venture on this curvy, flat road.

Ahead is the townsite of Irving. And 1½ miles farther, Prairie Road ends, merging with Highway 99. Just before that juncture is Maxwell Street. Turn left here, in the direction of River Road. At River Road turn right, using the specially marked bicycle lane, and return to Skinners Butte Park.

Skinner Cabin, Skinners Butte Park

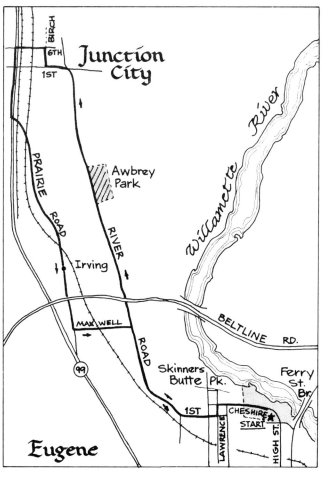

General location: Springfield and east
Distance:
  short route: 15 miles
  medium route: 26 miles
  long route: 41½ miles
Riding time:
  short route: ±1½ hours
  medium route: ±2½ hours
  long route: ±4 hours
Traffic conditions: light
Road conditions: mostly level; a few small hills
Ride rating:
  short route: *
  medium route: ***
  long route: ****

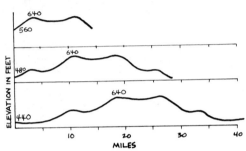

This tour allows you to start in three different places, depending on how many miles you feel like bicycling. You can start the long version at Island Park in Springfield, located along the Willamette River near the bridge connecting Eugene and Springfield. You can start the medium length version at the McKenzie River on Marcola Road near Town and Country School. Finally, you can bicycle a quiet and pleasant road along the McKenzie starting at Hendricks Bridge Wayside Park on U.S. 126.

All three versions wind along the McKenzie River and are nearly devoid of automobile traffic. Few rides in the Eugene area offer as much scenery and safety and easy riding as these options.

Start the long version at Island Park in Springfield, making your way to Hayden Bridge Road as indicated on the map. It is here that you begin to leave the city behind and have the opportunity to view orchards and semi-rural living.

At the point Hayden Bridge Road intersects Marcola Road, turn left to the McKenzie River. Straight ahead is Town and Country School. On the south side of the bridge is a parking site used principally by fishermen. Persons interested in biking the medium route can drive to this spot and park their cars here.

Across the bridge take the far right road, called Camp Creek Road. While bicycling along here, look for openings in the shrubbery to view the McKenzie. Impressive rolling hills and small ranches also dot the landscape.

Bear right at the intersection with Upper Camp Creek Road, remaining on the regular Camp Creek Road and continuing toward the McKenzie Highway. At Millican Road, leave Camp Creek, turning right. This little residential lane will take you close to Hendricks Bridge Wayside.

This park, with its wooded, grassy grounds, is a fine site for picnicking, fishing, or wading in the icy McKenzie. It also is the starting point for cyclists interested in the short version. The easiest way to reach it for people driving from Eugene-Springfield area is to head east on U.S. 126 until reaching the McKenzie.

Cross over to the south side of the river and bicycle east along Deerhorn Road. A few secluded homes are located on the banks of the river, and further on, the beginnings of a resort-type subdevelopment. But despite these urban "intrusions," Deerhorn Road is extremely pleasant bicycling.

The pavement eventually ends, but not before Deerhorn County Park, located along the river on Bridge Street, across from a golf course. A fine place to stop, rest and picnic.

To return, follow the same roads as before. It is possible to cross over the bridge to U.S. 126, but the traffic is heavy and the scenery is in no way comparable to Deerhorn and Camp Creek Road.

Deerhorn County Park

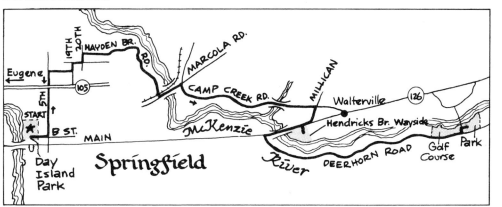

The Oregon Coast

42 FT. STEVENS PARK LOOP

General location: Astoria area
Distance: 14 miles
Riding time: ±1½ hours
Traffic conditions: light
Road conditions: level
Ride rating: *

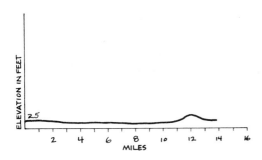

If you have never bicycled on an ocean beach, you absolutely have to take this tour, which is located just outside Astoria. The trip starts in Fort Stevens State Park, a few miles west of Astoria (many signs direct the way). This enormous park is something of a marvel in itself, once one realizes that the lush vegetation all around came about through a massive sand stabilization project in the 1930s. Photos on a bulletin board near the camp headquarters illustrate the progression from sandy wasteland to a region overgrown with grasses, shrubs and trees.

An ideal starting point within the park is along Coffenbury Lake, a small sand basin lake surrounded by picnic tables and lawn. You might also want to explore nearby Crabapple Lake and "Creep and Crawl" Lake, smaller marshy ponds accessible by bicycle.

After cycling around the park, take the road to the beach (a sign shows the way). At the end of the road is a parking lot and tracks through the soft sand made by motorists driving on the beach. Walk your bike to the packed, wet sand, the part of the beach licked by ocean surf.

Directly ahead are the rusty remains of the British ship, Peter Iredale, driven ashore here by a heavy storm in 1906. Over the years the ship has deteriorated, and all that is left are the ruins which you see before you.

From the ship head north along the beach. Ride only on the packed sand, as close as you dare to the incoming sea. You will find the surface not quite as hard as asphalt, but solid enough for relatively easy cycling. As you ride up the coast you probably will see both fishermen and seagulls waiting for a nibble, clam diggers with buckets and shovels in hand, and sand dollars galore. And, always, there is the constant drone of the ocean in the background, its spray in the air.

Before you know it, the 3½ miles of beach riding will have come to an end, and you will have reached the rock jetty stretching out into the Pacific, separating the ocean from the Columbia River. Here again you will have to dismount and walk across the soft sand, following one of the several paths made by beach drivers. Once over the sand embankment, there is an asphalt road leading south from the jetty back to Ft. Stevens Park. Along the way is the cracked concrete shell of Battery Russell, the only site in the Continental United States fired upon during World War II by a Japanese submarine. It is an eery place to visit, standing where sentries once looked out over the ocean in search of Japanese vessels.

In another mile you will come to a fork in the road. The right-hand section will take you back to the park entrance less than a mile away. The left-hand road will take you into the old Fort Stevens grounds. They are worth visiting to see the once stately buildings and blocks of streets now engulfed by blackberry bushes.

Bicycle around some of the back streets of the fort, but when you are through, head toward Hammond, taking the road adjacent to Ft. Stevens Junior High. In a short distance is a four-way intersection — the town of Hammond. To the left is the Columbia River, more ruins of the Fort, and the horn you have been hearing all day, sounding out its warning to Columbia River shippers. To the right is Ft. Stevens State Park.

Wreck of the Peter Iredale

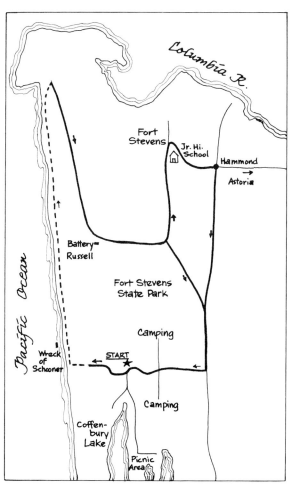

43 FT. CLATSOP LOOP

General location: Astoria area
Distance:
  short loop: 16 miles
  long loop: 21½ miles
Riding time:
  short loop: ±1½ hours
  long loop: ±2 hours
Traffic conditions: light
Road conditions: mostly level
Ride rating:
  short loop: *
  long loop: **

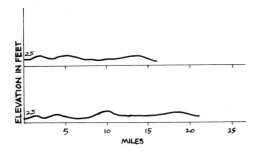

More than 150 years ago, overland explorers Lewis and Clark made preparations to spend the winter near the mouth of the Columbia River. During December, 1805, a small log dwelling was constructed just south of the present city of Astoria, named Ft. Clatsop after the Clatsops, a friendly local Indian tribe. These quarters served the 30-man exploration team until spring arrived and they returned home to report their findings.

The original fort disintegrated long ago, but a replica has been built in its place. The fort is now a national memorial and serves as an interesting stopping point for cyclists taking this scenic tour.

Start at Tapiola Park, located on the southern side of Astoria on Highway 202 near the high school. Cross the bridge spanning Youngs River, at the east end of Youngs Bay. At the intersection of Miles Crossing turn right. Cross yet another bridge, this one spanning Lewis and Clark River. At the next intersection, bear left in the direction of Ft. Clatsop. The fort, about a half-mile down the road, is part of a 125-acre wooded area and is interwoven with well-tended foot paths. The visitor's center contains many interesting exhibits and often presents slide shows on the Lewis and Clark expedition.

Leave the memorial site and bicycle south along the road by which you entered the area. It passes through farmland and river marshes, cattails lining the road. At the bridge crossing, some 4½ miles from the fort, you must decide whether to take the short or the long version of this tour. For the short version, cross the bridge and turn left at the intersection on the other side of the river. Follow this road back to Miles Crossing and to the starting point at Tapiola Park.

For the long version, do not cross the bridge, but continue bicycling south, on Lewis and Clark Road. On the downslope of this road there is an intersection with another road, Logan Road, switching back to the left. Take this road and follow it back to the bridge, to Miles Crossing, and eventually to Tapiola Park in Astoria.

Ft. Clatsop

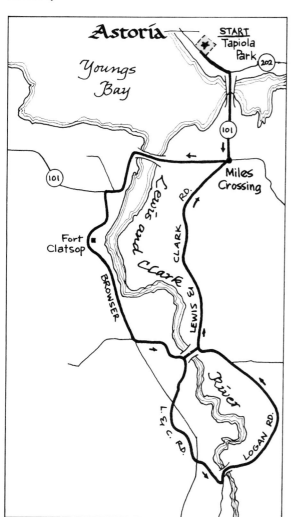

44 YOUNGS FALLS LOOP

General location: Astoria area
Distance: 23½ miles
Riding time: ± 3 hours
Traffic conditions: light
Road conditions: hilly
Ride rating: ***

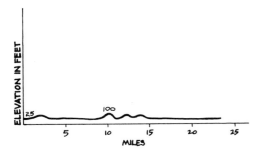

There is nothing quite like pressing hard, pumping, pumping, pumping up a climb, Douglas fir shooting skyward on all sides of you, the narrow line of asphalt winding its way up the mountain slope. Your brow becomes moist from the effort. Your legs feel like they have been stretched too many times. The palms of your hands begin to grow tender from gripping the handlebars tightly too long.

At the moment when all the exertion seems to be taking its toll, there is the summit, and the reward of rest. But on this tour there is more: Youngs River Falls Recreation Area. No finer place to dismount, walk down the path to the clear river pool below, the roar of Youngs Falls ever in the air. And such magnificent falls they are! White water cascading over a cliff a hundred feet up, crashing into the pool below, river mist creating almost a fog in this otherwise sunny canyon.

This tour is for bicyclists who enjoy the above sensations and are in the physical shape to manage the slopes. Start in Astoria at Tapiola Park, located on the south side of the city near the high school on Highway 202. Cross the bridge spanning Youngs River, at the eastern tip of Youngs Bay. At Miles Crossing, turn left and follow this road along the river valley. It's a lush area: farmland surrounded by mountains jutting upward, covered with layers of green.

About 10 miles from the starting point, beyond lumbering operations, backlogs of booms floating in the river, and windy, hilly pavement, is Youngs River Falls Recreation Area. Spread out and enjoy the lunch you packed. If you brought your fishing pole, start casting. A beautiful spot it is.

Leave the falls area and continue on the road toward Olney. At this townsite — gas station and grocery store on the corners — turn left onto Highway 202. The road becomes more and more level as it progresses into the valley — a real pleasure to bicycle. Follow it all the way back to Tapiola Park in Astoria.

Along Youngs River

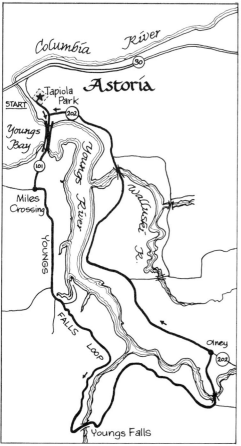

General location: Tillamook
Distance:
   short route: 15 miles
   long loop: 22½ miles
Riding time:
   short route: ± 1 hour
   long loop: ± 2½ hours
Traffic conditions: light
Road conditions:
   short route: level
   long loop: some steep climbs
Ride rating:
   short route: *
   long loop: * * *

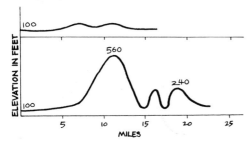

Tillamook probably means cheese to most people — and justifiably so. But there is more here than the famous Tillamook Cheese factory. There is Tillamook Bay and a flat road along it; there are forests and rugged climbs; there are magnificent parks and beach areas. All of this is located on this bicycle loop to the west of Tillamook, which takes in the towns of Cape Meares, Oceanside, and Netarts.

Except for the road along Tillamook Bay, however, this is not an easy loop to bicycle. There are some mighty steep climbs on the long version, especially up to the Cape Meares State Park entrance. But if you are in shape (or do not mind walking the steep inclines) this is a beautiful tour. The short version is completely flat and offers a nice ride around the bay to the ocean.

Begin bicycling at the Pioneer Museum, located in the very center of Tillamook. It shares the same plot as the Tourist Information Center and is situated at the intersection of Highways 101 and 6. Plan to spend some time going through this museum, either before or after completing this bike tour. It is filled with relics of the past: Indian baskets and beads, spinning wheels, early horseless carriages, and an old stage coach. There is also an outstanding natural history collection and marine relics.

Cross Highway 101 and turn left for one block to 3rd Street where you turn right onto Netarts Highway. Follow this road for about 2 miles to the Tillamook River, and shortly thereafter come to an intersection. Turn right. This road follows the shore of Tillamook Bay. After about 7½ miles of bicycling, you'll pass the Bayocean Peninsula and come to another intersection. The right-hand road leads to the townsite of Cape Meares, the destination of the short bicycle route. For this route, return on the same road.

The left fork leads toward Cape Meares State Park and Oceanside. It also takes you to several steep climbs, the first one being the most grueling. But bear with it, walk parts of it if you cannot bicycle it all. At the top is the entrance to Cape Meares State Park where the Octopus Tree is located.

From the park it's all downhill to Oceanside, and what a joyful ride! It makes the earlier climb very much worthwhile. Oceanside, like most coastal towns, has a few stores and a beachfront. Much the same can be said for Netarts (its name is said to come from a small Indian tribe which lived in the area) a little south of Oceanside. Stop at either of these places if you are in the mood for some salt air, sand, and ocean watching.

Just south of Netarts is the final climb and final intersection. Head straight, up the hill, in the direction of Tillamook. Follow this road back to the beginning of the loop, across the Tillamook River, to the Pioneer Museum in downtown Tillamook.

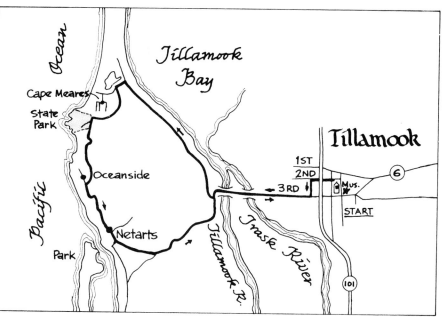

46 CAPE KIWANDA LOOP

General location: Pacific City
Distance: 16½ miles
Riding time: ±2 hours
Traffic conditions: light to moderate
Road conditions: mostly level
Ride rating: *

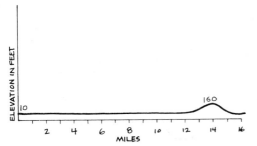

Salt air and sea breezes. Fishing boats resting on the beach, waiting for the day's catch to be unloaded. Sun bathers and sea grasses covering white sand beaches. These are some of the images of Cape Kiwanda, and all are a part of this short, easy-to-ride bicycle loop.

A good starting place is Cape Kiwanda itself, located just north of Pacific City, opposite Haystack Rock which juts out of the ocean just offshore. There is ample parking here and a lovely beach to relax on after the ride.

Head south on McPhillips Drive, continuing in that direction until reaching Pacific City in about a mile. Cross the bridge into the central part of town and take a left at the next intersection, heading in the direction of Woods. Again cross a bridge into Woods (about another mile down the road) and, after passing the center of town, turn right. This road is marked with a sign saying "Cloverdale: 4 miles," and is a quiet, narrow, windy road following the edge of the valley. It's a beautiful grazing area, the sights and smells of this industry very much in the air.

At Cloverdale, cross yet another bridge, with a white steeple church straight ahead. Turn right at the main intersection in Cloverdale and proceed south on Highway 101. Again, the road winds past dairy and farmland for about two miles, at which point you turn right in the direction of Woods on Pacific Road. This section of the route follows the Nestucca River.

At Woods, cross over the bridge you traversed earlier, thus completing one-half of this figure-eight loop. But this time, instead of turning right on the outskirts of Woods, bear left on Sandlake Road and follow the road in the direction of Tierra Del Mar and Sandlake. This sometimes hilly road passes through some wooded sections, the trees rooting themselves in mountains of sand dunes. In about two miles there is yet another intersection, with a sign indicating Pacific City to the left. Turn left and follow the road back to Cape Kiwanda.

Haystack Rock

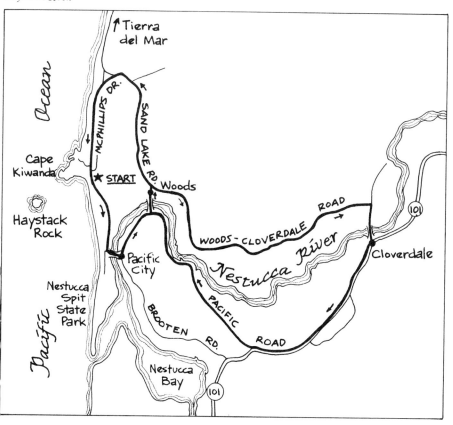

General location: Tillamook
Distance: 31 miles
Riding time: ±3 hours
Traffic conditions: light
Road conditions: level
Ride rating: *

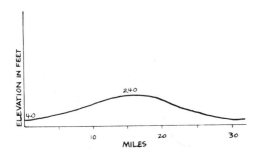

To really appreciate this trip to the fullest, strap a fishing pole to your bicycle, for the Trask River is definitely a fisherman's river. At the park situated at the end of this 15½-mile ride, fishermen seem to have no trouble hooking into whatever kind of fish are in season — trout, Chinook, or sometimes silver salmon. One time we saw three 14-inch trout netted in a five-minute period. Further down the river from the park is a big pool where, at the right time of the year, you can sometimes see huge black salmon lying near the bottom, motionless, waiting for the end of the last portion of their life cycle.

Start this route at the Pioneer Museum in downtown Tillamook, at the intersection of Main Avenue and 3rd Street. Bicycle east on 3rd, which soon becomes the Old Wilson River Highway. Avoid the newer route, Highway 6, which is north of and parallel to the older route. Follow the Wilson River Highway past the fairgrounds to a four-way intersection. On one corner is the Fairview Grange; on another is the old Fairview School. Turn right onto Trask River Road. In another mile and a half is a second intersection, just before a bridge. Trask Road leads off to the left.

Follow this relatively flat road to the edge of the Tillamook Valley and through a ravine in the mountain range ahead. Surprisingly, the road remains nearly flat; the ups and downs are nothing even the three-speed bicyclist will be concerned about. To the right of the road is the rocky bed of the Trask River.

About 15½ miles up the road is a park, complete with camp sites, picnic areas, restrooms, and of course the Trask River. Should you need to buy anything, the townsite of Trask and its general store are another mile up the road. (The road soon turns to gravel just beyond Trask.)

For the return trip, follow the same road back to Tillamook.

Trask River

Tillamook

General location: Tillamook
Distance: 14½ miles
Riding time: ±1½ hours
Traffic conditions: light
Road conditions: level
Ride rating: *

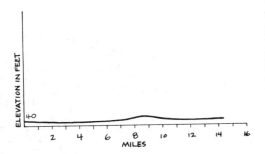

Have you ever seen cheese made? Do you know the difference between sharp and mild cheese? This loop provides a chance for you to see the process and taste the difference. Tillamook is blessed with a world-renowned cheese factory where you can observe the cheese-making process daily. But this loop also allows you to view some of the other necessary parts of the process: dairy cows grazing on fertile grassland, and dairy farms where the milking — both by hand and by machine — takes place.

Start this loop at the Pioneer Museum in downtown Tillamook, at the intersection of Main Avenue and 2nd Street. Head north on Highway 101 for about ¾ mile until reaching the cheese factory on the right. The highway has a wide shoulder and is generally not busy along here.

After viewing and munching some Tillamook cheese, bicycle south on Highway 101 for a few hundred yards until reaching Latimer Road. Turn left onto this road and follow it past some of the dairy pastures. At the three-way intersection 2 miles down the road turn right onto the road leading to Tillamook and Route 6 (a sign indicates the direction).

Cross Route 6. You'll be able to see the dome of the Fairgrounds building straight ahead, where you will turn left. Continue to the Fairview Grange intersection and turn right. Follow this road past the Trask River Road turnoff, across the Trask River and around past Tillamook County Airport, where you will see giant hangars that housed the coastal patrol blimps in World War II.

This road, called Long Prairie Road, eventually crosses Highway 101, becoming Hunt Road, and bends northward back to Tillamook. Remain on it until reaching a three-way intersection with an auto repair shop on the left-hand corner. Highway 101 is a few hundred feet to the right. Return to it (called Pacific Avenue within the city) and bicycle north the few remaining blocks to Pioneer Museum.

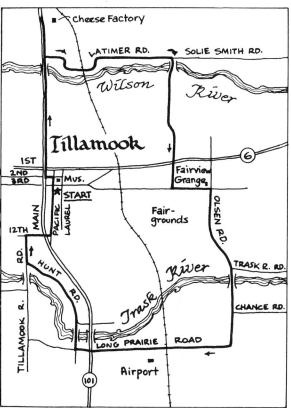

49 YAQUINA BAY LOOP

General location: Newport
Distance: 23 miles
Riding time: ±2½ hours
Traffic conditions: light
Road conditions: few hills
Ride rating: * *

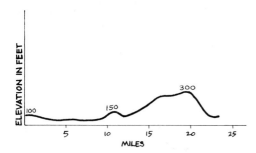

This ride is a must for those people who enjoy the windy roughness of the ocean, the peaceful calm of a bay, the solitude of a lonely road, and an invigorating hill or two — all "rolled" into one bicycle loop.

Starting point is Yaquina Bay State Park in Newport, located on the north end of the landmark Newport bridge. There are many wind-sheltered picnic areas and cooking facilities in the park for your before- or after-ride meal. The lighthouse, situated on a knoll in the park, has a small museum worth visiting, too. The fascinating legend about its being haunted is worth reading.

Head east toward the bridge where you will encounter a fork in the road. Bear right and go under the bridge, winding downward into Newport's bayfront. Here you'll pass by fishermen hauling their day's catch onto the pier, colorful sidewalk fish markets, mountains of circular crab traps, and row upon row of boats silently waiting for the next venture out into the Pacific.

Continue on S.E. Bay Boulevard beyond Newport's city limits and up a slight incline, onto what is now called Yaquina Bay Road (same road, different name). Soon you'll pass lumber mills operating almost alongside oyster farms.

The one-store town of Yaquina and a little farther, Winant, soon are passed. (The word Yaquina, incidentally, is the name of a small Indian tribe that once roamed this area.) By the time you reach Winant, the road will be almost free of traffic.

As you follow the road around the bay (which eventually becomes Yaquina River) you will come to Boone Point, the place where Daniel Boone's great-grandson settled in 1852, becoming the first white man to live in the area. You will also encounter the only significant incline on the route, just south of Toledo.

Soon, off to the right, will appear a gigantic lumbering operation. That is Georgia-Pacific's spruce plant, which during World War I was government-owned and supplied spruce for manufacturing airplanes. Now it is simply known as the world's largest spruce sawmill.

At the first junction in Toledo, turn left, onto Highway 229. This is the road which takes you back to Newport. After about a mile there is a much larger junction: Highway 20 intersects Highway 229. Turn left again. This road can be fairly busy, but it has a wide shoulder bicyclists can use with safety.

A gentle, mile-long rise begins shortly after the junction, but it is not difficult. Shortly after the top, the Old Corvallis Highway intersects Highway 20, just west of Benson Road on the left. Turn right on the Old Corvallis Highway and you will once again leave the traffic behind. Continue to wind down into Newport. There is a great downhill section along here.

After passing the fairgrounds on the right, the pavement becomes gravel. Remain on it for a few blocks more until you reach Highway 101. Turn left and, at the next intersection (Olive Street), turn right and head for the ocean. In ten more blocks you will have reached the beach scenic route, where you turn left, following it back to Yaquina State Park.

Yaquina Bay

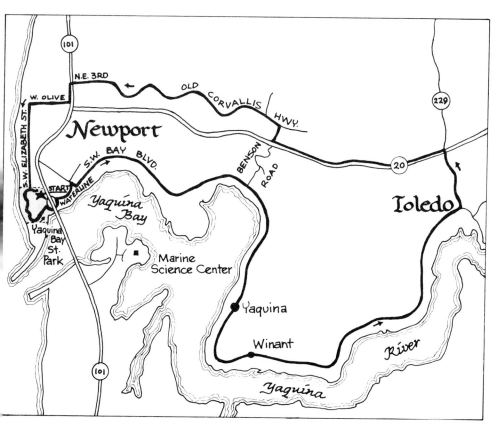

50 DEVIL'S LAKE LOOP

General location: Lincoln City
Distance: 10 miles
Riding time: ± 1 hour
Traffic conditions: light
Road conditions: mostly flat
Ride rating: *

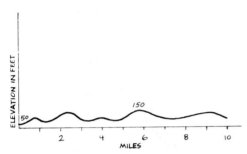

in the direction of the sign saying "City Park." After traversing a short climb, you are away from the mainstream of traffic and alongside Devil's Lake. Follow Devil's Lake Road until it once again intersects Highway 101. Turn right here and continue on to Neotsu, a wide spot in the road with a green and red post office. Turn right again, but bear left at the fork in the road just after Highway 101. This intersection is decorated with clusters of brightly painted signs indicating who lives where. In about a mile is Viewpoint Loop Drive leading off to the right toward a small, lakeside county park. It's worth the detour to this site for swimming and picnicking.

For the rest of the loop, follow the main road around the lake, stopping off at East Devil's Lake State Park if you like. The name of the lake, incidently, comes from an Indian legend which has it that an evil marine monster would occasionally surface and devour unwary tribesmen.

Once leaving the State Park, head toward the intersection with Highway 101, turn to the right, and return to 'D' River Wayside.

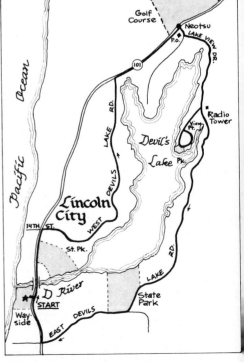

This nice, short, but sometimes hilly, route loops around the very scenic Devil's Lake in Lincoln City, about 45 miles south of Tillamook along the coast. It is an ideal tour for people who don't want to bicycle very far but yet are interested in some solitude and natural settings.

The best place to start is at the 'D' River Wayside, just south of the heart of Lincoln City. Ample parking is available at this beach front, as are quantities of driftwood for collectors.

Bicycle north on Highway 101 into Lincoln City, turning right on N. 14th

GARDNER
CAIN
HOYT
BELL
BROOKMAN
SAM A. ANDERSON
MYERS
FOSTERS
The ANDERSONS
LOKTING →
THE HARA
NAMITZ
FREERKSEN
Jujimuras >

DRAYTON
KIPVER
WEAVER
WRXUGG
DUTTON
ROSE
Erickson
MC COMB
NOTTINGHAM
BRINKERS
HEIDER
KEAN >
HALL
RICE >
CALVID
KELLY

General location: south of Lincoln City
Distance:
   short route: 18 miles
   long route: 33½ miles
Riding time:
   short route: ±2 hours
   long route: ±3½ hours
Traffic conditions: light
Road conditions: mostly level
Ride rating:
   short route: **
   long route: ***

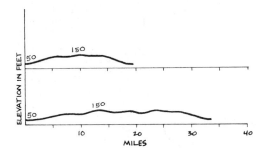

Five miles south of Lincoln City is Kernville, what may seem on first glance not exactly an illustrious site for much of anything. But if you turn left, toward the Siletz River on Route 229, in about a mile you will find a strangely familiar 19th century house situated on the opposite bank of the river. There might be a river tug moored in front. And sometimes you might even see people commuting across the river, the only access to the house except by rugged hiking.

This is the house that was used in the filming of Ken Kesey's book *Sometimes a Great Notion*, and is now the private residence of a genuine logging family. The tug also was a prop in the movie. But the river and surrounding scenery were here before Hollywood set up shop. Even if you have not seen the movie, you'll want to come here, bicycle this road along the Siletz River, and enjoy the magnificent countryside first hand.

A good starting point is across the river from the "Great Notion" house, where there is ample parking. Bicycle eastward along Highway 229. The route involves some hills, but none that is outrageously steep. More than some occasional hills, though, is the striking beauty

of the land that impresses one. Branches of trees arch over the road in places, old dock pilings jut out of the river, and sunbleached stumps and dead tree trunks stand out on hillsides of new growth. About two miles along the way is the site of the original Kernville, named after Daniel Kern who settled here in 1896. being one of the first white settlers in the area. He built a fish cannery at this site which Lincoln County claims was the first industry within its territory. A little farther on is Medicine Rock, a spot where Indians would leave presents for good luck.

About 9 miles from the starting point, the pavement ends. This point makes a convenient stopping point for those riders interested in a relatively short ride on paved road. But for bicyclists who want to go farther and don't mind negotiating hard-packed gravel (it is almost like asphalt in some places), there is a quiet park 7 miles up the road. (There are only 4 miles of gravel; the rest of the way is paved.) Jack Memorial Park is located along the Siletz River and offers picnicking, camping, fishing, and river swimming. The return trip is along the same route.

Hank Stamper House, Siletz River

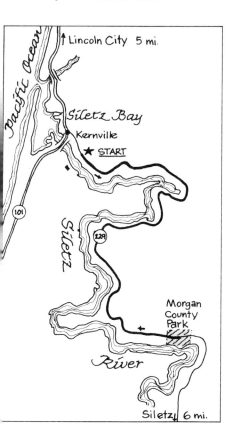

Lincoln City 5 mi.

Pacific Ocean

Siletz Bay

Kernville

★ START

101

Siletz

129

Morgan
County
Park

River

Siletz 6 mi.

52 FLORENCE-HECETA BEACH LOOP

General location: Florence, Central Oregon
   Coast
Distance: 14 miles
Riding time: ± 1½ hours
Traffic conditions: light
Road conditions: level
Ride rating: *

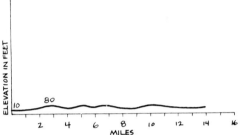

Sand dunes have a special fascination; rolling hills of white, barren except for the most rugged of shrubs and trees. They are, of course, impossible to bicycle on, and almost impossible to hike. But Florence has a quiet, paved road cutting through a section of sand dunes along the ocean toward Heceta Beach. It's beautiful in its barren, wasteland starkness, and when it is not windy, it is also pleasant to bicycle.

Start from the Old Town section of Florence, near Fisherman's Wharf, as suggested in the Florence to Minerva Bike Route. Turn on to Highway 101 and head north for a few blocks until you reach Rhododendron Drive. Turn left here and follow this street to the beach. It soon angles right and parallels the beach. The name of the street changes to Coast Guard Road after about a mile.

If you see seagulls circling off to the

right when you are absolutely certain the ocean is off to the left, that is because the nearby garbage dump is more productive than the sea for these flying scavengers. Also nearby is a dune buggy rental, in the event you want to explore the sand dunes on four wheels.

After 4½ miles of sand dunes and wind-blown shrubs and trees, you will come to a junction. Turn left toward Heceta Beach. At the beach is a small, somewhat sheltered park with picnic tables. There is also a modern, seemingly windowless hotel complete with heated indoor swimming pool.

The beach and nearby Heceta Head were named after the Spanish explorer, Bruno de Hezeta, who sighted the area in 1775 while searching for the Northwest Passage. The pronounciation of the name of the beach, incidently, is as if the word were spelled *Heseta*, accent on the second syllable.

To return, follow the Heceta Beach Road, but instead of turning off at Coast Guard Road, continue straight until reaching Highway 101. Turn right on the highway and bicycle a little more than half a mile on it. At the junction with Munsel Lake Road, turn left. This is a much smaller, quieter road which leads to Munsel Lake, a nice place to stop and relax.

Continue on this Munsel Lake Road until it ends at the intersection with North Fork Road. Proceed on North Fork Road to Highway 126, the Eugene-Florence Highway. Turn right toward Florence, bicycling for about one-half mile, until Highway 126 crosses Quince Street. A left turn here will take you back to the Florence Old Town section where this tour began.

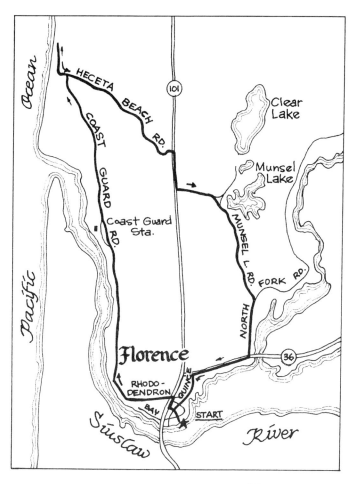

53 MINERVA ROUTE

General location: Florence
Distance: 24 miles
Riding time: ±2 hours
Traffic conditions: light
Road conditions: curvy, flat
Ride rating: **

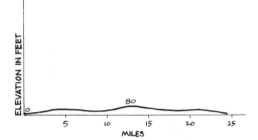

Florence has sand dunes and beach buggies and wind and rain and sun and sea. Sometimes all at once. But what most people do not know is that Florence has an easy access to mountains and forests and valleys, all sheltered from salt spray and gusty winds.

One such access is the road to Minerva. This road is becoming a very popular route for local bicyclists. A convenient starting spot is the Old Town section of Florence, near Fisherman's Wharf, along the Siuslaw River. Begin bicycling along Laurel Street, which becomes 2nd Street, which again becomes Quince Street, until you intersect the Florence-Eugene Highway, Highway 126. Turn right onto this main thoroughfare, heading toward Eugene, keeping well on the shoulder part of the road.

In less than a mile, North Fork Road intersects Highway 126, just before the North Fork of the Siuslaw River. Turn left on this road. Follow it for another mile until reaching a "y" with Munsel Lake Road leading to the left and North Fork Road bearing right. Go right.

Now follow the road to its eventual end. Along the way you may see old sagging barns, herds of cattle grazing in the valley, farmers feeding their chickens, and, late in the afternoon, young boys bringing in the cows for milking, all in single file.

The pavement and bicycle route end at a covered bridge. This site is called Minerva, named after the wife of its first postal official. No post office is there today, however. Return to Florence by retracing the same route.

Road to Minerva

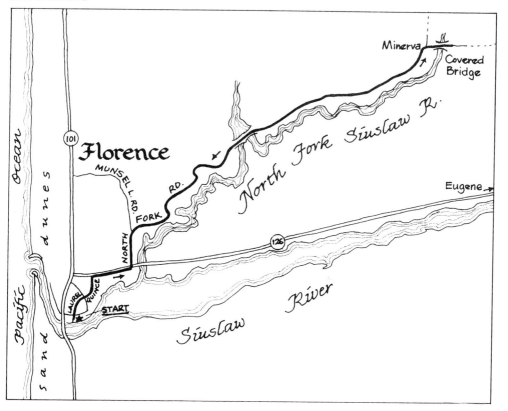

General location: Florence
Distance: 16½ miles
Riding time: ±1½ miles
Traffic conditions: light
Road conditions: hilly
Ride rating: **

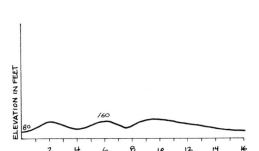

onto a road leading to Woahink Lane. There are more campgrounds along here should Honeyman Park be full. Continue along this road, up and down its slight hills, across a narrow bridge spanning an inlet of the lake, and past an intersection with Clear Lake Road. This intersection comes after about 1½ miles of bicycling from Honeyman Park, and Clear Lake Road serves as the return route.

But for now, keep pedaling straight, along this road bordered by conifers, brush and wild flowers. After a few more inclines you will cross railroad tracks and begin the steepest climb of this loop. Shift into your lowest low, for this is no easy climb. But it is only one-half mile long, and down the other side is Canary, the destination of this loop.

Coasting down the hill, you'll come into a clearing of what used to be a booming region. All that remains are a few cottages and trailers, a U.S. Mail railroad car, and the still operating Canary Trading Post, its shingle exterior painted an appropriate yellow.

Around the bend are the remains of Canary's once major industry: a log pond and a wigwam burner. According to a local resident and former mill worker, the place was shut down "because of the environmental thing — too many little regulations the mill couldn't meet."

Leave Canary by the same road you entered, but when you reach Clear Lake Road, about 3½ miles from the Canary Trading Post, turn left. This area is considerably more developed than the Canary townsite. Summer homes line the road, some of rather distinctive architecture and others of no more distinction than that which is provided by the manufacturers of mass-produced mobile homes.

Clear Lake Road eventually crosses Boy Scout Road. Turn right, remaining on Clear Lake Road. A short distance further, "Darling Loop" intersects Clear Lake Road. This short detour to the left provides a view of Siltcoos Lake, and takes you by a store and a boat launching site.

Return to Clear Lake Road and turn left in the direction of Highway 101, which is a few hundred yards down the road. Turn right on Highway 101 and bicycle back to Honeyman Park. There is a wide shoulder on this highway which bicyclists may use with safety.

The Florence area is filled with beauty and contrast. This trail portrays some of each by taking you to a deserted logging town, a resort lake, and along mountains of sand.

Begin this loop at Jessie M. Honeyman Memorial State Park, located about 2 miles south of Florence on Highway 101. The park is a pleasure in itself, sand dunes surrounding it, lush vegetation, and a sandy bottom pond reserved for swimming. The picnic areas and cooking shelters are plentiful and spacious.

Leave the park and cross Highway 101

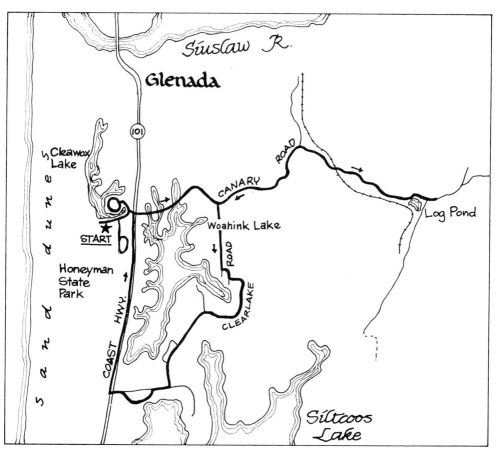

General location: Florence
Distance: 11½ miles
Riding time: ± 1 hour
Traffic conditions: light
Road conditions: level
Ride rating: *

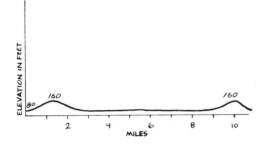

Of the two bicycle tours that originate at Honeyman Memorial State Park, this one is by far the easier to pedal. There are no inclines along the route, which follows South Jetty Road. The road is as flat as the ocean beach which it parallels for most of its length. Traffic is almost nonexistent along the road since it dead ends at the tip of the jetty. And the scenery consists of sand dunes as far as the eye can see, with hardy grasses rustling in the ocean breeze.

Begin bicycling at Honeyman State Park, located some 2 miles south of Florence on Highway 101. Leave the park and bicycle north on Highway 101. This is perhaps the most difficult part of the route: sometimes the traffic is heavy and there is a slight climb. But the road has a wide shoulder bicyclists may use, and the turnoff for the jetty is only about 1½ miles from the park.

A large sign indicates South Jetty Road off to the left. Turn on to the road and leave the traffic behind. There are some turnouts along the way equipped with restroom facilities. You can park and lock your bicycle and climb over the sandy embankment to reach the ocean.

At the end of the road is an old dock used by pole and crabnet fishermen. Driftwood abounds. Seagulls, standing in the surf, wait for a meal to swim by. The grasses and shrubs murmur messages only discernable by the shifting sand.

To leave this beautiful spot, return on the same road back to Honeyman State Park.

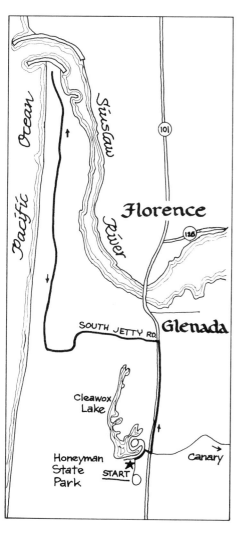

Pacific Ocean

Siuslaw River

101

Florence

126

SOUTH JETTY RD. **Glenada**

Cleawox Lake

Honeyman State Park

START

Canary

Cleawox Lake

127